THE ZUNIS
Self-Portrayals

THE ZUNIS
Self-Portrayals

BY THE ZUNI PEOPLE
ALVINA QUAM, Translator

ALBUQUERQUE
UNIVERSITY OF NEW MEXICO PRESS

© 1972 by The Pueblo of Zuni. All rights reserved.
Manufactured in the United States of America by the
University of New Mexico Printing Plant, Albuquerque.
Library of Congress Catalog Card No. 72-86817
First Edition

Foreword

In 1965 the Zuni tribe, using funds allocated by the Office of Economic Opportunity, made plans to record their oral literature. The major storytellers of the tribe were gathered and asked to relate on tape the legends, myths, and history of the Pueblo. Thus has been recorded the entire body of literature of one of the most interesting tribes of this hemisphere.

In 1968, Dr. C. Gregory Crampton of the Duke Indian Oral History Project at the University of Utah joined with the tribe to support the translation of this material. The recording and translation were managed at the Pueblo by Quincy Panteah. As Alvina Quam began translating the tapes, it was immediately apparent that the material had great cultural relevance, so those of us connected with the Duke Project and the Zuni High School placed some of these legends in the school where they could be used for educational purposes.

Using money from the Bureau of Indian Affairs, Research and Cultural Studies Development Section, headed by Dave Warren, the Governor and Council appointed Mrs. Virginia Lewis to review and edit the legends, stories, and tales with an eye to publication. The final choices were approved by the Governor and the Council. Representing the Center for Studies of the American West, University of Utah, and the Duke Project, I have had the pleasure of working with the Governor, the Council, Mrs. Lewis, Mr. Panteah, and finally with the University of New Mexico Press. Everyone involved in the project has taken great care to preserve the cultural integrity of the Zuni people as presented in this book. Indeed, the book is the work of the Zuni people. I have been flattered that they would accept my small role as coordinator of efforts to bring this fecund and colorful body of literature to their friends and the public at large.

Floyd A. O'Neil
Assistant Director
Center for Studies of
the American West

Introduction

First fruits of a harvest arrayed in the center of a room—the family gathered around for the ritual of Thanksgiving.

The man and son, taking the store of piñon nuts gathered by a pack rat for winter eating—replacing the "take" with an equal amount of grain.

The man and son, with cornmeal, saying a prayer asking the "Keeper of our life's road" to replace the young Christmas tree they will cut.

Simple things—good things!

Prophecies of old, told by the old to the young—coming true. The do's and don'ts for a long and good life.

Briefly, this is the way of my people.

Stories told with morals attached, characters, whether fictional or true, that symbolize these ways have kept us together so long.

We are proud to present this, the first volume of stories told by the oldest members of my Zuni people, for your reading enjoyment—the old and young, in classroom or home.

Robert E. Lewis
Governor, Pueblo of Zuni

CONTENTS

Foreword   v
Introduction   vii

I   SOCIETY

1. Prophecies of Our Grandparents   3
   drinkers of dark liquids will come
2. Zuni Witchcraft   4
   the funnel of wind stopped
3. Sacred Way to Hunt Deer   6
   after offering pollen they laid the trap
4. Henry Hunting Deer   8
   to my terror, the buck lifted me up
5. Ed Vanderwagen and the Bears   12
   he knew bears to be sly and tricky
6. Woodcutter: Enote   18
   they kept their fires going
7. Story about Nutria and Ojo Caliente   19
   they were a lively people
8. The Two Orphans and Their Grandmother   27
   the Fire God came to the door
9. Zuni and Their Ways of Living   36
   it is for our children to decide

II HISTORY

10 Poorest Days of Enote: Enote   41
    we grew up hungry
11 The Return of the Zuni Slave Woman   42
    they walked all night
12 The Navajo and She-She's Wife   51
    then was a time of hatred and vengeance
13 Raid before Coming of the Shalako   57
    they rose up with a war cry
14 Spirit World of the Zunis: Enote's Trip to   65
   Koh-thlou-wah-la-wah
    there came a flock of white geese
15 Famine in Zuni   66
    the Zuni land was but a waste land
16 The Zuni and the Apache   68
    he picked them off one by one
17 Mexicans Who Captured a Zuni Man   70
    he enabled himself to cast spells
18 The White Shoomehcoolie   72
    the Yellow Ant was summoned
19 Zunis and the Outlaws   75
    the Indians were stronger than any white man
20 Zunis and the Outlaws   86
    the Zunis lassoed Red Pitkins's horse

III FABLES

21 The Coyote and the Badger   93
    he did not feel the mice chewing on his fur
22 The Whip   98
    the whip uncoiled itself and looked out
23 The Ghost   101
    the shadows began reflecting monstrous images

Contents

24 Turkey Maiden — 107
    long ago the world was young and soft

IV FABLES OF MORAL INSTRUCTION

25 The Priest's Son and the Eagle — 111
    the boy and the eagle flew away
26 Little Arrowheads — 115
    they were afraid of the memory
27 The Grasshopper and the Coyote — 117
    she heard the grasshopper singing
28 A Coyote and a Bumblebee — 121
    the ears of the coyote were all burned

V RELIGION

29 The Beginning — 129
    the children became small animals
30 Two Girls and the Dancers — 137
    the girls stayed with the Kachinas
31 True Way of the Scalp Dance — 140
    a man knew within himself
32 Matsakya — 144
    the Kachinas transformed themselves into birds
33 Priest's Son and the Spirit World — 146
    he saw a white feather standing
34 Yellow Water Serpent's Head — 170
    the yellow streaks of light pointed
35 The Capture of the Runaway Shoomehcoolie — 179
    the figure came floating through the forest
36 The Zuni Dances — 180
    the Salimobiya circled the village
37 Adventures of the War Gods — 182
    the heart flew to the sunset

38 The Rituals of Hunting	194
the men would not pass the four days	
39 Priest's Son and the Grandmothers	197
the rains will always come	
40 The Cloud Swallower	202
their grandmother the bear heard this	
41 Story of Salt Lake	205
the Salt Lady did not like being polluted	

VI WAR AND DEFENSE

42 Lonkeena and the Horse Thieves	209
an Indian is hard to kill	
43 Zunis and the Navajos	231
the Zunis prepared their weapons	
44 The Navajo Warrior Kethlnakai	232
Tzuni atop his white horse came bounding	
45 Doowhooli	237
Zuni do not think of themselves during battle	
46 Apaches Raid Zuni	242
a lone house sat ablaze	

MAPS　　　　　　　　pages xiv–xvii

ILLUSTRATIONS following page 38

THE ZUNIS
Self-Portrayals

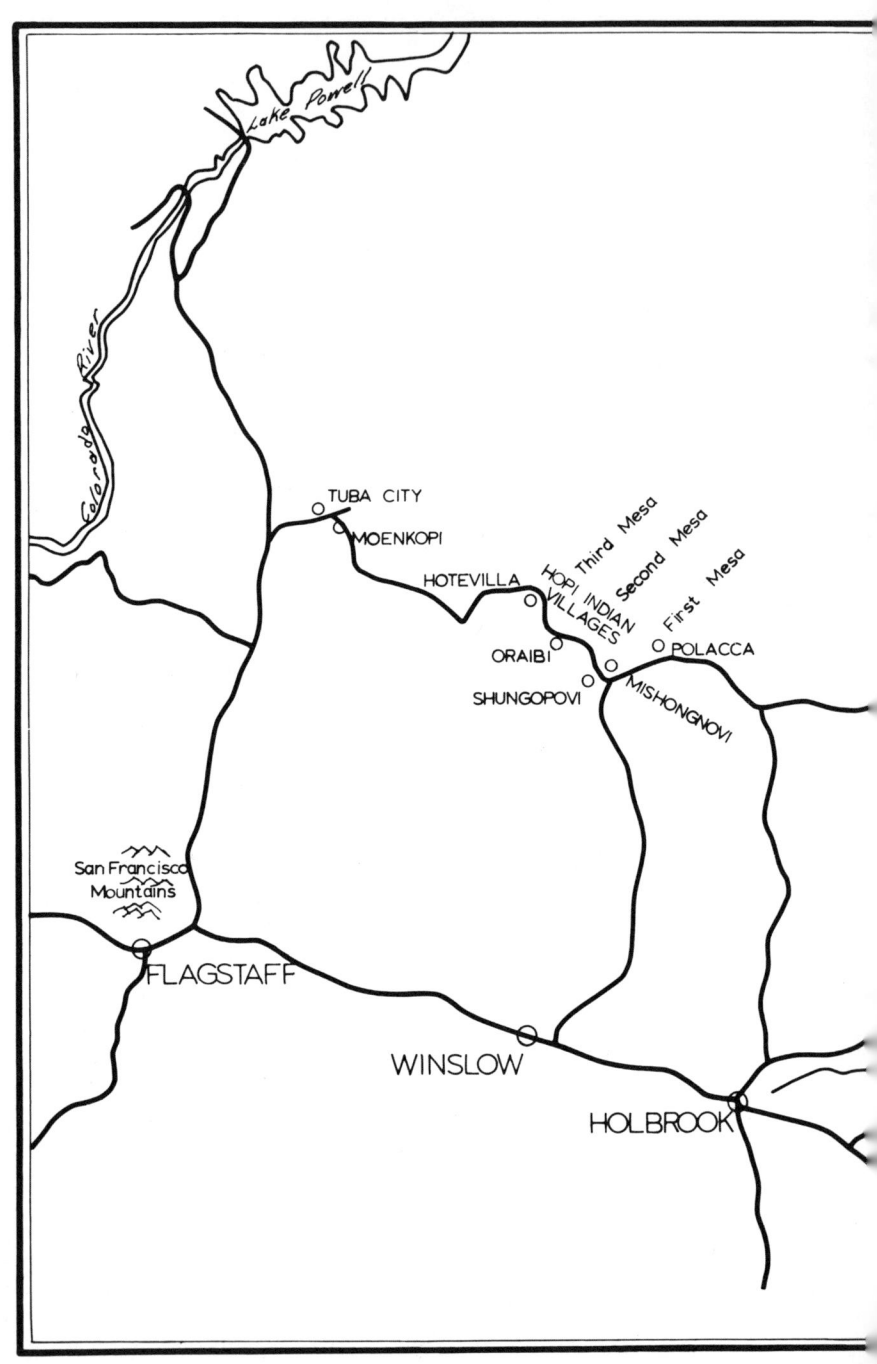

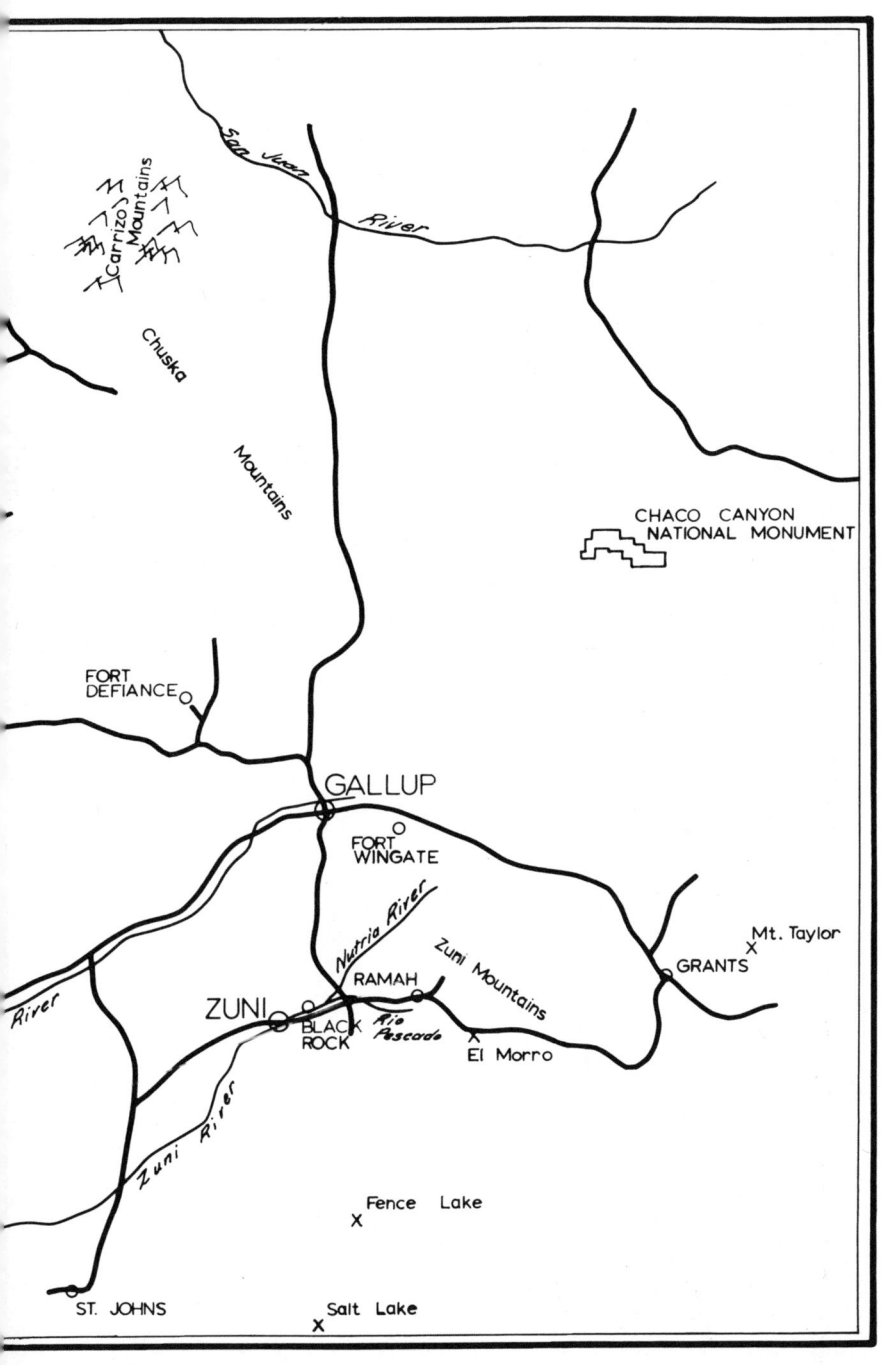

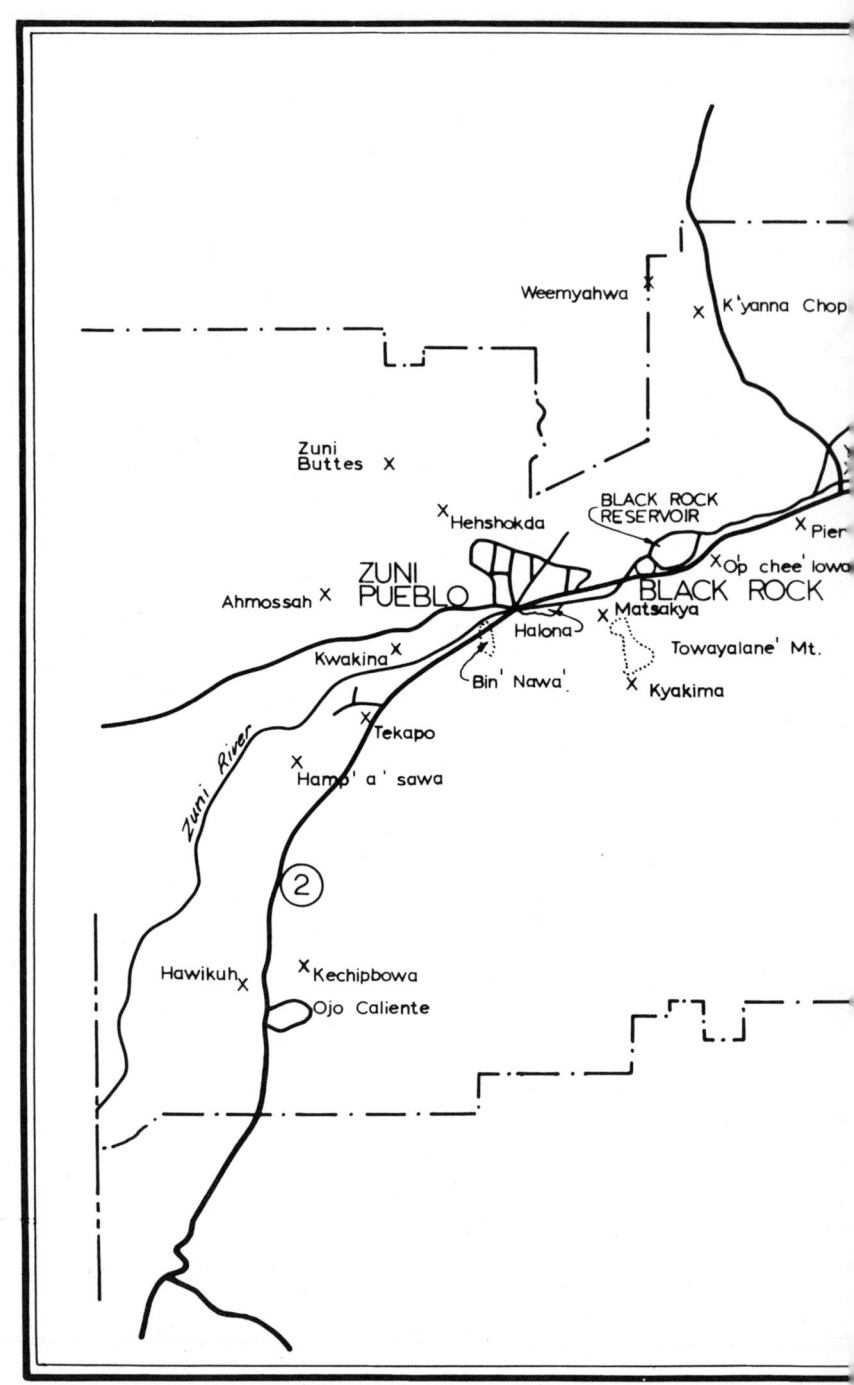

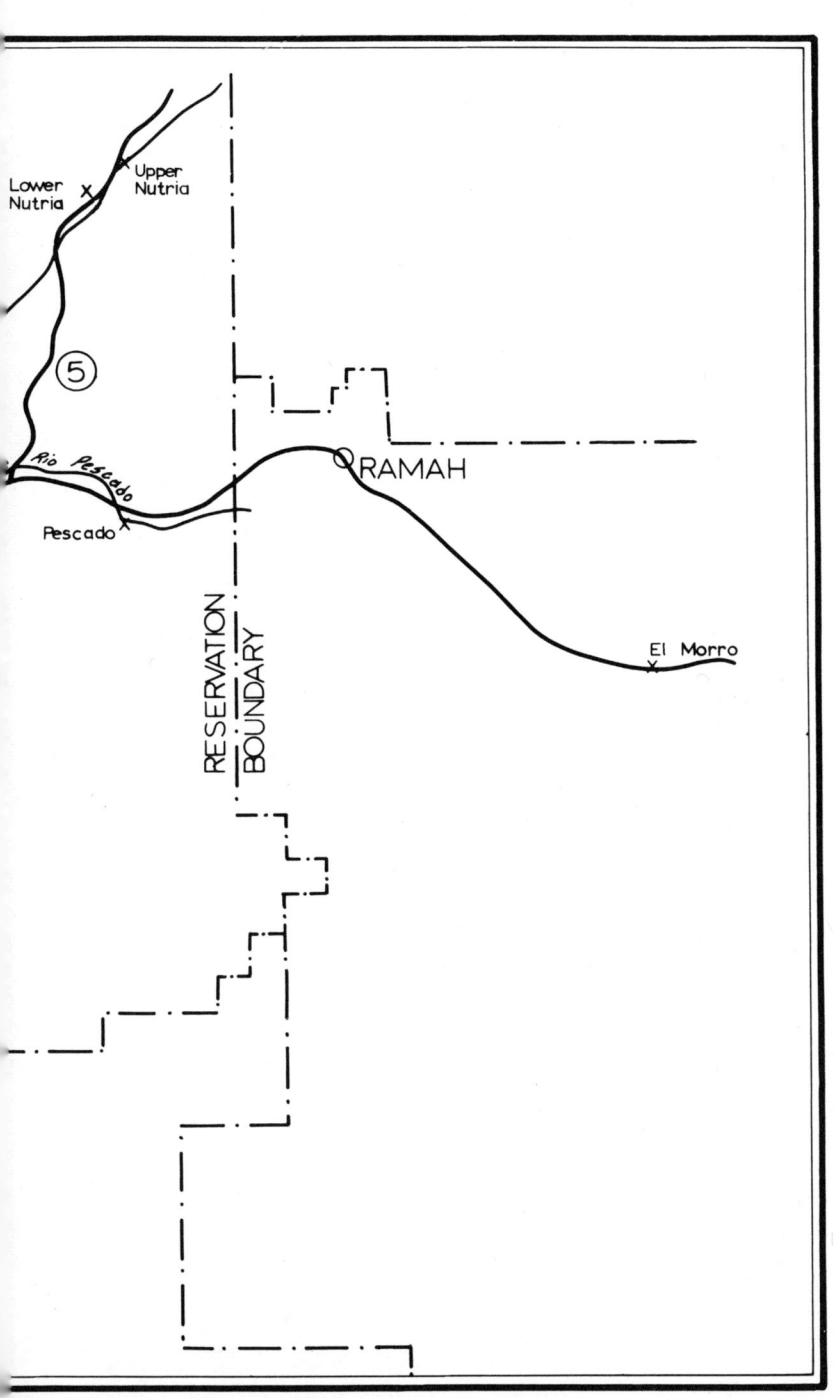

I SOCIETY

1 Prophecies of Our Grandparents

Many years ago when our grandparents foresaw what our future would be like, they spoke their prophecies among themselves and passed them on to the children before them.

"Cities will progress and then decay to the ways of the lowest beings. Drinkers of dark liquids will come upon the land, speaking nonsense and filth. Then the end shall be nearer.

"Population will increase until the land can hold no more. The tribes of men will mix. The dark liquids they drink will cause the people to fight among themselves. Families will break up: father against children and the children against one another.

"Maybe when the people have outdone themselves, then maybe, the stars will fall upon the land, or drops of hot water will rain upon the earth. Or the land will turn under. Or our father, the sun, will not rise to start the day. Then our possessions will turn into beasts and devour us whole.

"If not, there will be an odor from gases, which will fill the air we breathe, and the end for us shall come.

"But the people themselves will bring upon themselves what they receive. From what has resulted, time alone will tell what the future holds for us."

2 Zuni Witchcraft

In about the middle of autumn when the rains came abundantly, a person not in his right senses, called a witch, went about the shrines of Ahauda, praying for them to stop the rain.

First he went to the shrines of Towayalane and prayed to the images of the Ahauda that they would stop the rain.

In about a month interval, he went to Hanging Cotton, where he prayed again.

At that particular time, a man returning from hunting in the east sat down to rest, tying the horse's legs and putting the deer he had killed on the ground. When he again sat down, there came a gush of wind, followed by a small funnel of wind. It stopped short of the tree where the man sat watching. When the funnel of wind stopped, amidst it, there stood a person, the man named A-wah-gon-neh, the witch. He looked about as if looking for someone. But he acted as if he could not see anything.

Each time he stepped in the whirlwind and started to whirl, it would whirl a few times and stop. When he had done that several times, the horse hobbling about came a little way from the tree and A-wah-gon-neh saw it. He looked closer and saw a man sitting under the tree, so he approached him.

"Hey, what are you doing way out here? I am doing a sacred ritual, but it will not work because you are watching."

"Oh? Is a religious person supposed to walk around prepared the way you are? You wear yucca around your ankles and across your chest. And the owl feathers, why are you wearing these things? You are one from the witch society. Our fathers spoke many times of the powers of the evil ones."

Society

A-wah-gon-neh did not rely, and the man asked, "What are you doing anyway?"

"It is the rain that brought me here. I do not want rain. I first went to Towayalane to the shrine, and to the Hanging Cotton, and I was getting ready to go to the east shrine of Twin Buttes, when you discovered what I was doing. But now I am finished, I cannot use my powers any more."

"Are you positive? Are you sure you will not continue to be a hindrance to your people?"

"No, I will not do anything else."

"Well, I shall go now."

"Yes, you go on ahead, I will follow shortly."

The hunter left as A-wah-gon-neh sat himself by a sagebrush. He hurried into the village, going directly to the house of the Bow Priests. He told them of what he had seen. Then he went on home.

The Bow Priests waited until A-wah-gon-neh returned home. As soon as he did, he was literally dragged from his home to the Bow Priests' residence.

He asked why he was being treated in this manner.

The Bow Priests told him of the information received about him. When they confronted A-wah-gon-neh with the accusation of being a witch, he did not deny it. He confessed that he was out at the shrines praying to the Ahauda to stop the rain from coming, assuring the Bow Priests that he would not do anything again, as he had been discovered at his evil ways.

The priests could not do anything, so they let A-wah-gon-neh go free. They waited until the season of the rains came; then the man's assurance was made well known.

The rains came and the fields were green with an abundance of crops growing and the streams ran, overflowing into the fields, helping to irrigate.

3 Sacred Way to Hunt Deer

When our grandfathers went out to hunt deer, the rituals they went through to make themselves able to hunt with great results were begotten through the beliefs of many elders.

Sha-nah-dewa, my grandfather, who lost his father during one of the Navajo raids, lived near the south side of the village.

As he grew up to be a young man, his stepfather taught him the ways of hunting and the ways of the Zuni men. So his stepfather announced one day, in envy of the other village men, that perhaps they would go out and hunt for some deer. But first, the father had to go out and find a possible rooting place of the deer. It took one day for Sha-nah-dewa's father to locate a place where they possibly could kill a couple of deer.

He came back and prepared himself and his son to go out to Dethle-ya-kyan-hah, meaning to prepare a trip to help themselves get a deer or two.

Food was prepared and packed for them and soon they were on their way into the forests. Coming into a tall-pine-studded area, along the foot of some mountains, they went on until they came to a new growth of oak trees where prints of deer were in abundance. There they measured a space about two-and-a-half feet by eight feet, there they built a small shelterlike ditch, about two feet deep, upon which they laid several thin poles, then covered the openings with grass, twigs, and dirt.

A few feet away they tied some twine to trees around the area where the ditch was. Then they left their trap after their prayers to the gods, and after offering pollen they laid the trap.

For the next three days, the men checked on their trap to find if they had caught any game. After the third day,

Sha-nah-dewa's father awoke his son early and announced that his dream the night before had been a good one. He believed this day would be a very good day; maybe there was deer in their trap.

Soon after their morning meal, the men packed a meal and rode onto the south edge of the plains a distance from their trap. There they tied their pack mule to a tree and walked on.

From still quite a distance, they ran to their trap when they saw the deer in it. They saw it when they noticed the antlers out from the head.

Shouting with delight, they came running down the hill. With the rug they had prepared the ditch with, the men snuffed out the last breath of life from the deer.

They held the rug tightly around the head and soon it fell over dead. Then the men dragged the dead deer out of the trap, and putting it along a pole, they lifted it to their shoulders and walked down to the place where their pack mule was standing.

They immediately dressed the deer, cleaning it and quartering the sections. When they grew hungry they sat down and ate, and again after the meal they returned to their trap to find another deer. So they got this one and did the same things they did to the other deer.

They prayed again and left with their meat. When they reached their homes, the meat was dried and stored away.

For three days they left the trap unchecked and on the fourth day they went back, finding another large buck. They killed the deer and took it home.

For many days after they used the same trap to catch deer. When the animals became familiar with the trap, they then moved it to a different location.

During these times, the Zunis had meat in abundance and were never hungry as long as they had deer meat to supply their needs.

4 Henry Hunting Deer

Many years ago, when I was young and spry, I used to go out hunting deer. Each year, when hunting season opened, I went out on my horse with only a gun.

This one year I went to Nutria, scanning the mountains and canyons. I had a hard time spotting anything until I started back. I was coming along the edge of a mountain, and down below in a gully separating the mountains I saw some bucks, roving around in some brush munching on leaves.

I dismounted and went down into the gully. The deer went around a corner, coming toward me, then turning into another gully. The three were large bucks, trotting slowly until they saw me. The two up front were swift and agile as they ran into the heavy forest, while I shot at the last one, which was a pretty good sized buck with four points. I shot it in the stomach and it cringed. I shot it again as it ran over a little hill coming down to a wash. Nearby under a tree the buck fell, with its insides clearly visible.

I came after it, resting my gun against a tree. I ran down into the wash. When I reached the buck, it had lifted itself and was sitting in a crouched position. Sure that it would be an easy task to finish the buck off, I thought of how I tackled live sheep, bringing them down while the sheep fought with all their strength but how helpless they were. I was confident of my strength, so I grabbed the antlers, and to my terror, the buck lifted me up as it stood up and I fell to the ground. Then it ran off with all the speed of an unwounded buck. It ran over a hill going to the west as I sat up on my knees. I was ready to go after it as I picked up large pieces of stone, ready to hail stones upon it, when I realized what I was doing; thinking of the incredibility of anyone bringing down a buck from a bombardment of stones.

As I came up on the hill, the buck was going straight into a deep gully heavily forested. Disheartened, I decided I would come back the next day with Naboowahghah. I turned back and picked up my gun, mounted my horse, and came on home.

That night, little drops of rain fell all through the night, and I was telling my grandfather about the buck. He enthusiastically agreed to come along the next day.

So early next morning we saddled our horses and went off to Hohshodahgosque. Before we reached the place where I had left the buck, from a small hill the tracks of two large bucks led down into a canyon. They were only a couple of hours old, so I exclaimed to Naboowahghah, "Let us go after these two. They should not have gone very far. If we hurry we might each get us a deer. We will wait until tomorrow to go after the one I shot yesterday."

Naboowahghah agreed and we were off. We dismounted and tied the horse reins to a tree limb and ran on following the clear trail. But when we came to a mound of rocks, the tracks separated, showing the one going toward the mountains and the other going straight forward. So I asked my grandfather, "Which one are you going after?"

"I will go after the one going south."

"All right, do not make any mistakes."

I left after the one headed west on across a gorge into the forest. As the tracks led to the foot of some mountains, the tracks came back together. Just as I came upon the meeting place, grandfather appeared at the edge of the forest. I called to him and asked if he had seen the buck at all, and he replied, "The tracks are leading to where you are."

"Yes. They have gotten together again. Let us go now. We will go after them up the deer trail. They must have gone up."

So we went after them again until we reached the foot of the mountain, where the trail led to the top. Here, the tracks showed the bucks had paused a moment, and then one left a trail going farther south with the other headed up along the trail. "I will go see if the deer is going up. If so, we shall track it down," I said to Naboowahghah and went after the deer.

I ran a short distance and found the tracks going farther up, so I returned to grandfather and said, "It is going on up. Let us go after it."

We went up the trail, pausing every few minutes to catch our breath. As we came close to the top, there was a wide ledge; above started the mountain of jagged rocks and cliffs with some areas of sleek sheet rock. We followed the tracks to another ledge where the deer had laid down for a while.

It was almost mid-noon and the sun was directly overhead, making our pursuit harder. Naboowahghah examined the cliff carefully and found tracks going into a shallow cave. From there, the tracks turned to the west onto another trail. I decided to check up farther before going on, so I left grandfather and went up. I came to a trail going down into a gorge full of brush and trees. I went on down and only a few feet to the west the gorge spread out into mounds and hills. The trail was fresh and clear as I kept to it. As I came out I could see grandfather above me, and he too noticed me down below. I motioned him to come down, as I was sure the buck was not far from where I was. When he came down I told him I was going to follow the tracks as they came within nine feet of grandfather into a deep gorge.

I was excited as I told grandfather to wait once more while I went in after the deer. I went in a few yards when I spotted the buck with the four points with its head bent down, eating the leaves of a small bush. It was chewing.

I took aim and shot, hitting the head. The buck leaped almost the same instant it was hit. It leaped onto a large pile of rocks, onto another where the brush covered it from me. Grandfather came running in, as the buck came from behind the brush and leaped down toward me. It came down about nine feet from me, and I shot it between the shoulder blades as it fell.

Grandfather came yelling and asking where the buck was, so I answered him and he was upon us in a few minutes.

We cleaned the insides out and then pondered how we could get the buck down. We were still some distance up on a ledge, below the one where we first discovered the deer tracks descending to where we were now.

We skirted around the ledge and found only a narrow path. So I suggested that grandfather go down and get the horses and keep them below the ledge, and I would shove the buck down off the wall of sleek rock.

Grandfather went down. As soon as he called up to me that he had tied the horses nearby, I took the buck by the antlers and dragged it to the edge of the cliff. It was none too easy a job, for the buck was heavy. I pushed it off and it rolled down along the side of the mountain into a gorge full of brush and twigs.

I hurried down the narrow trail and came to my grandfather. Together we went in, and grandfather took the buck by the antlers; I was surprised at the strength of the old man as he pulled the heavy buck out to a small clearing. I helped him drag it farther.

We took a rope and tied it around the antlers and then tossed the rope over a tree limb. Then we lifted the buck until it was a few feet off the ground. We had the horse under the limb and carefully lowered the buck upon the horse's back. Having tied the buck securely, we started out for home. The following morning we started out again into the forests, onto the mountains, and we came to the place where I had shot the first buck, but the tracks had been washed away by the rain. We wandered around the area a bit before we found tracks made recently by the wounded animal.

The tracks led into a deep gorge onto a little wash, where we came upon the buck eaten away by some other animal. We decided one buck was enough to feed our families with, so without hunting further we came on home.

5   Ed Vanderwagen and the Bears

North of Zuni where Ed Vanderwagen, who was a white man, once had a store near some Navajo settlements, a man came to him one morning complaining that a bear had been ruining his corn crop. He came to Ed to ask for help in getting rid of this bear. Ed asked where the bear was and what its size was. When the Navajo told him, he packed his mule with his weapons and they started out for the place where the man had last seen the bear.

They came to the foot of the mountains, and the Navajo pointed out a small cave where he had seen the bear enter. As they came closer to the cave they could see the bear lying against the wall of the cave. The Navajo exclaimed to Ed that he must leave before anything happened to him. He left Ed standing near the entrance to the cave and returned to his cornfield.

The Navajo happened to be deathly afraid of the bears, as they believed the bears were supernatural beings and were capable of casting evil spells over the Navajos.

Ed stood for a moment wondering what he should do. Then he picked up a large stone and threw it into the cave, hitting the bear. In an instant the bear stood and Ed aimed, shooting the bear in the neck. The bear dropped to the ground and then got back up. Again Ed shot the bear, this time through the face. The bear dropped and did not get up again.

As Ed waited for the bear to rise again he sat himself on a ledge to watch it. When the bear made no move Ed took a stone and threw it down, hitting the bear. The bear lay still, looking dead. Ed would not come any closer, for he knew bears to be sly and tricky. He thought the bear might be pretending. He threw a couple of other stones, and when the bear still did not move, Ed took his mule and led it down into the area where the bear lay very still.

Ed took his rifle and shot the bear once more to make sure it was dead. When he was sure the bear was dead he had his mule help him hang it from a tree branch and then skinned it. Then Ed quartered the bear, bringing the meat over to the mule to pack on his back. At the smell of the bear meat Ed's mule ran away, going into a ravine and on out of the same canyon they had just entered. Ed left his meat and went after the mule. But when the mule saw Ed coming for him, he started snorting and bucking his hoofs.

From above, where Ed had shot the bear, came another white man going through the canyon. When he heard noises down below him, he looked down to see Ed struggling with his mule and shouted down at him. Ed recognized the voice and immediately called to the man asking for help, and the man responded and came on down. When he reached Ed they held down the bolting mule and packed it with the bear meat. When they had strapped all the meat on the mule they let it stand a minute. With Ed holding a strap in front and the other man holding one from behind they pulled the mule, trying to get it to come forward. Instead the mule bolted, rising up on his hind hoofs and jumping around. The two men held the mule until it finally settled down. Slowly they made their way out of the canyon and home.

They came home and sold the meat to customers. For three weeks the meat lasted before it finally sold out. The Navajo would not take the meat and there weren't that many white people around the place to buy it.

A day later another Navajo came in complaining about bears getting his crops. The Navajo had seen two small cubs and had chased them into the forest, where they had climbed a tree. Ed again started out, this time taking his car, with a saw, some ropes, and of course his weapons. The Navajo took Ed to where the cubs were and left him there. The cubs were at the top of a tall pine tree. Ed threw a rock and some wood up in the tree, trying to get them to come down, but they would not budge. Then he took his saw and began to cut down the tree. As the tree fell the cubs clung tightly to the limbs, and they fell to the ground and the tree fell on top of them. Ed thought both cubs had been killed. He hauled them to the car and put them into the back seat. He started from the forest, but only a short distance from where he had loaded the cubs into the car, he thought he heard breathing. It was coming from the back seat. He slowly turned around to take a look. He saw a bear's paw coming up onto the front seat. He jumped out, opened the back door, and pulled one of the little injured cubs out. Then he struggled to open the door, which the other cub had pushed closed. The cub got itself tangled in a bunch of rope, so Ed tied its feet and paws, then tied it to a tree. He checked to see if the other cub was all right, but to his surprise, he discovered that it was dead. He went to the store and got another man to come with him and help bring the other cub in. They made a small cage with fence posts and wire mesh. They brought it back and let it stay outside the house for a time. Ed kept the bear for some time.

As it grew bigger, Ed's son, Ernie, played around with it, until one day Ernie stuck a nail through the wire mesh and poked the nostrils of the bear. The bear let out a growl and struck Ernie with his claw, cutting a gash on his face. Ed heard Ernie scream out in pain and ran out to find his son with blood dripping all over his face. They kept the bear only for a short time longer, then sold it to a store owner in Blue Water.

Later on, near Cedar Creek, Ed had a store but left it to come to Zuni to live for a while.

Ed and his wife, Dena, liked hunting deer, so when hunting season opened they took their friend Dominic and camped out for the night. The second day Dena left, telling them to stay put until she came back. She went out a short distance for a breath of fresh air. As she sat down to rest she saw a deer and took careful aim at it and shot it, killing it with only one shot. She ran back to camp shouting her news, "Come help me, I just killed a big deer!"

The three ran back to where Dena had shot the deer. Sure enough the deer lay dead. Dominic checked it and found it was a doe. Quickly they took the deer back to camp and dressed it. They quartered the meat and hid it under the car seat. They were sure no one could find it there.

They sat down to supper and after, Ed told Dena she must go back to Zuni during the night. Dena was frightened and didn't want to go alone, so Dominic offered to bring her back to Zuni. They decided that Ed would come behind them until they got to Black Rock, where Dominic got out of Dena's car and Ed picked him up. Then Ed and Dominic went back up north into a small canyon. They split up and each walked along the foot of the mountain and on up to the top. They went in about a mile and then Ed stopped to rest. He heard two shots from the opposite side. As he looked into the canyon down below, from a cave came a huge bear, standing with his paws spread out looking around. Just as the bear's gaze fell on him, Ed took a shot and hit it. The bear pawed himself and fell, then stood up and walked as a man, coming after Ed. Its left shoulder was down, while the other stuck out as if it were reaching for something. Ed turned around and ran until he came to a tall pine tree and climbed up to the highest limb. He was perched there as the big bear came up a rise and looked about for him. The bear backed away a few feet, then jumped onto the tree and slowly made its way up to a limb close to where Ed sat. As the bear climbed onto the limb it cracked, then broke. The bear fell to the ground, facing up, and Ed shot it right through the heart. As the bear lay there having convulsions, Ed came down from the tree and stuck it with his knife. As the bear lay bleeding, Ed watched it until the body became still. Not knowing what else to do, he stood there looking at it for a long time. Then Dominic came running through the bushes to him. Dominic looked down at the bear and cried out, "Hey, what have you got there?"

"I had to kill it or it would have killed me," replied Ed.

"Did you get anything? I heard two shots."

"Yes, I killed two bucks not very far away from here," replied Dominic.

"What are we going to do first?" Ed asked.

"Leave the bear here and we will go after the deer. It will not take too long," Dominic suggested.

They went back a mile to the car and soon were heading into the canyon, finding their way along over a small hill. When they could not go any farther, they walked to where the deer lay. They brought the deer back to the car and dressed them. When they finished, they sat down and ate a meal, then started out for the bear. When they reached it they skinned it. Dominic wanted to start back home, but Ed wanted to rest and then go look for wild turkeys.

Dominic was satisfied with his deer, so gave no thought about going anywhere else. Ed had gone out looking for a possible roosting place for turkeys. He came upon a place where bunches of willows grew beneath the trees. There he found some large white eggs. He went down to investigate and found the eggs were turkey eggs. He went back just above a small canyon and set up a place where he could spend the night. Then he went back to Dominic and told him to wait there until he returned.

Ed went back to his little campsite and waited for the

turkeys. When dark was just beginning to fall, about half a dozen turkeys came to their nesting place. Ed was waiting and ready to take as many as he could. He did get all of the half-dozen. He took word to Dominic and had him help pack the turkeys into position on a tarpaulin. Then they returned to Zuni.

Ed and Dominic had a time making jerky and eating all of the meat they had brought.

Many other times they killed game and gave out all the meat to their people, and the Navajo and Zuni remembered these people for their generosity.

6   Woodcutter

A story told by Enote and translated by Alvina Quam

Many years ago, during a very hard snow in Ojo Caliente when it was freezing cold, a man went to gather some wood. His donkeys were out someplace, so he just took a rope and his axe and went up into the forest not far from his house. Gathering the wood, he placed it on a rack. Hauling the wood down, he found it to be heavy, so he decided to leave his axe behind and come for it later. So he went on, stopping to rest only once. He finally reached home, took the wood down, and went after his axe.

This was one of the ways the people made their living, and the way they kept their fires going.

7   Story about Nutria and Ojo Caliente

Many years ago, when the village was settled, the people went out looking, searching for places to start their fields of orchards and farming. In every part of the land, where sand was loose and fine, there grew rows and rows of apple, peach, and plum trees.

But today, to the south, the orchards have long since been laid waste, and to the west, there still stand a few fruit trees, cared for by the old men who live at their orchards the year round.

When the fruit was ready to harvest, it would be picked, some prepared in containers and other dried. When this was done, everywhere rows and layers of peaches would be seen drying out in the sun, on rooftops, some hung on fences. But since the new generations have come, there are no remaining ways of the old.

When there were but a few mules, men would haul wood upon their backs in order to have wood supplies to keep their families warm. They would take the limbs of oak trees and make a rack to hold the wood in. When the pack could no longer hold any more wood, it would be placed on the back of a mule with a strap, which went around the forehead, keeping the rack resting upon the back.

Our forefathers were indeed strong, physically and mentally. They walked everywhere. There were only a few mules during those times. It was not long before mules became plentiful on the land. Then little by little, things were made easier.

As people began to explore their countryside, they found many good fertile pieces of land. There sprung up the small farming clusters of Nutria, Pescado, and Ojo Caliente, and fields were soon planted with seeds of corn, wheat, melon, and beans. None who had founded the settlements remained. What elders we have now are not aware of the founders of their lands and homes.

Degyah, Coowehehsee, and Kalewueh were the first to own "Weyyessi," a plow, handmade with strong poles tied with tanned leather to the slabs of rock, first used as cutting implements. Then with the limbs of trees, they made little forklike implements, having sharp prongs, used to loosen the earth or cover the seeds planted. There were no horses at all, but when a new area was found good enough for growing crops, the people who owned the handmade plows were asked to plow the land and plant the seeds, with payment of food, which was eaten during the day of plowing and planting. There were no ill feelings among the people to keep them from helping one another. If it was a small field that could be leveled with a hoe, the men did not hesitate. They went on and plowed it with their hands and whatever tools were available to them.

Then came horses, and a new plow was made that could be hitched up to the horses, and plowing was made still a little bit easier. With the help of the horses, the men made dams along the rivers coming from the lakes. The dams made possible easier and faster irrigating, and the hard life was broken through. More food was made available, people were happy to work much harder and see what their efforts produced. The little farming clusters were populated year round; only at times of feasting or ceremonies did the people come into Zuni. Once the rituals were over, they would once again commute back to their farming settlements. As life became easier, more dams were built and people worked harder to improve their living conditions.

They were a lively people. They could not stay unproductive. And their social lives were rich and colorful. Many social dances were held in each farming village, or the exchange of dances between villages enabled people to knit relations closer together. Each time a new dance was created it would be invited to take place in one or all the villages; the War Bonnet Dance, the Buffalo Dance, and many others. A man in Pescado announced his desire to dance and have a feast, but could not possibly do it by himself. He would need help, as far as the food was concerned. He was then told that he would not be left by himself to shoulder all the responsibilities, but that the people were eager to participate in any social event. He was then asked what the dance was to be. He chose the Ba-h-kich-koh and preparations started immediately. The men who were to dance took only a short time before they were ready to commence dancing. They were the first ever to dance at Pescado. When the feasting was finished, after a short interval, the people from Pescado again announced a date for another dance. But before the dancing started, all the people had to be consulted in order to find out if there would be enough people to take part and enough food to be contributed for the feasting. When everyone gave their approval the preparations got under way, and soon the Hehmahdahtsi Dance was danced. The same night there was to be some more Navajo dancing.

The plans were made. Among the dancers were two men, Mogo-a-dinnah and Halashkah, who had earlier stolen some horses. They had been discovered at their theft and were pulled out of the dancing and confronted with the accusation in public. They confessed and told the people of how they had stolen them and where the horses were hidden. As it was time for feasting, the council men lectured the two men and set them free. All that time the dancing had gone on uninterrupted. But at the remembrance of thefts that had taken place, a man confronted another, Ohlohmah, accusing him of rustling cattle. He too was lectured.

"You, Ohlohmah, have been known to rustle cattle. If you are ever caught it will not be good. Why do you want to continue your way of living?"

He did not deny but instead spoke with anger, "Because of my hunger for meat. I am not the only one who does that. You, yourselves," pointing an accusing finger at the council members, "council men, with white men also, steal cattle from one another, butchering and eating the flesh."

"Hey! Who does he think he is, telling the council off, are you going to take his insults without fighting? Why don't you whip him!" a man angrily shouted to the council men.

"Yes! Go ahead and whip me. I didn't steal any cattle from anybody. Are you standing up for the white men who took them? Go ahead and whip me. It will not hurt forever," retorted Ohlohmah.

The man had at first replied kindly but soon denied having anything to do with rustling cattle. He spoke unafraid, standing up to the council.

"Is this all now? There is dancing going on and this is all ridiculous. Why doesn't everyone leave the council? Let them whip me!" Ohlohmah left the crowd and walked to the dance. No one ever bothered or accused him of anything again. He had told the truth when he said he did not rustle any cattle.

The festivities all went as planned and soon passed. The

excitement died down a little, before the people wanted another social gathering in Pescado.

They chose the Yah Yah Dance and decided they would tell all the other clans and have them make new songs for the dances. But they had a problem getting anybody to head the dancing groups. They finally decided on Weahkee and Unaidi to lead them. The two exclaimed, "Sure, we will do it. There is nothing to it."

Some women were chosen also, and soon preparations were made. The two council men from Pescado came to Zuni, informing the clan members to start making songs as the dancers were getting ready. Again dancing commenced and a great many people turned out, feasting and making merry.

A few days later, in the fields of Nutria, the corrals had been blown down and the men were repairing them when one man spoke up.

"Why not have a dance in Nutria? Everyone else has been dancing and we have done nothing."

Only a couple of days later, the council, Ohmsatte and Gho-gho decided to speak out to their people to gather to arrange and prepare plans to carry out their desires to dance and feast. So the people gathered and soon decided on a dance to be held near the home of Tsitsinah, for he had first spoken of what he wanted, and also because he had a large herd of sheep with which he could feed the people.

Tsitsinah approved of the plans but wished there could be some help with feeding the people. Soon it was agreed that the dances would be held and the problem of picking out leaders was discussed. Tucson and I were sitting by a fireplace in a corner when Kallestewa volunteered to lead the dance, with us the leaders, and soon everyone in the crowd began prompting us to agree.

Owaleson spoke first, "I will not lead the dancers but will follow my brother, Tucson."

So when Tucson agreed to this, the rest volunteered. There was Naiha, Be-selth-kaya, Noo-he-he, Be-thla, Na-gya-wan-nah, Hey-yeh-de, Kallestewa, Laate, and Kooshnah.

When all had agreed to dance, they agreed to come and meet several nights to practice their Navajo dance. The next day, Gho-gho did not want to go alone to Caliente to tell the people that two days before the dancing started they were to come to Zuni, so he got Na-thlup-kin-nah to accompany him. It did not take long for them to get to Caliente but they waited until night fell before they gathered the people to tell them their instructions.

"Tomorrow the word for feasting and dancing shall be given. There are to be three groups of dancing."

Immediately the people from Caliente formed a group of their own to join in the dancing. Chu-yate, Leyyew, Walela, Nalotsi, Iule, Ghahate, Tsadialusi, Coweuca, Dalaseyya, Angya, Sinitsa, and Lucanmi, with Boonshi as their Yeibichai, formed the group to go to Nutria.

Lanyate, Cheama, Delya, Namdonnah, Luhi, and Walu formed another group, with Tsamdawueh as the Yeibichai. Then Nogohha, Commah, Atdahtsanah, Namsoquah, Nihi, and Coocooba also formed one group.

They were all instructed to wait until two days before the feast day to come into the village. Then in Zuni, the people were told that they were to wait for the rest of the dancing group; also that to the south side of the village near Nutria's Ash Clan's house, in Cheama's house, they were to rehearse their dancing. A few days before the feast day, Lanyate was thrown from his horse, being injured so that he could not carry out his role as the leader for his group, and was replaced by

Hoonky. When the day came for the dancers to meet, they gathered at their designated places. Then the dancers supplied each other with the costumes and jewelry. Then the leaders were gathered and instructed as to who was to dance, and when. The dancing commenced. The group from Nutria came first, then from Ojo Caliente, and then from Zuni. When the dancing stopped the governor spoke.

"Now we shall go to our homes. The first thing tomorrow, you who are from Nutria shall go first to the Pine Tree Ridge and work on the offerings for your fathers. We shall come later."

"It shall be then."

Once more each group danced to one song, then went on home. The next day, offerings of prayersticks were prepared for the fathers. When that was done, the men inquired about a house to be at their disposal where they could carry out the rituals of completing their offerings.

They were given the use of a house at the center of the village on top of a hill. There the men gathered and the villagers were to come with food to serve. The men in the meantime were completing the rituals. When the offerings were finished that night, dancing commenced, lasting all night. Throngs of people came from other tribes and excitement filled the air, making people happy and free.

Then to the house where the people were to be fed came meat—dried venison, beef, mutton, and pork—which was contributed to feed all the people who wanted to eat. Tsitsinah, who had been the instigator of the feast, was to lead the dancing groups to his house where they were to be fed. In the middle of the night when the fires were lit in the plaza, Tsitsinah led them in a couple of dances before leading the dancers into the house. They finally went to eat; when they were through the dancing groups took turns dancing, never stopping.

When morning came, they were told to keep dancing until the sun was shining brightly overhead. It was mid-morning before the dancing came to a stop and the dancers wearily went to the house where the offerings had been prepared. There Nawehshe came and greeted all the dancers.

"How are you, my children? I have come with words. You will not end your dancing here. You must come to the center of the village, where you will dance once more."

"That shall be. But now we must rest a bit."

Meanwhile, there was to be a race between two horses, one from Pescado, a brown stallion, and another. They were to race in the morning so the dances could continue in the afternoon. The people gathered at the river where the race was to start. There was betting everywhere, mostly for the stallion. Nawehshe was riding it and Halate was riding the other.

They started following a long trail. The trail went to Pescado on around a grove of trees. Back to Nutria the horses came, and as they rounded a bend, the stallion was ahead, but only a few feet behind was the other horse. The horse running for the Nutria people was small but very fast. It ran as if there was someone chasing it. It came nearer to the crowd and excitement was clear. Shouts and cheers pushed Halate and the small horse. A few feet from the end, the stallion was passed and joy leaped through the crowds. Then slowly the people drifted back into the village and the dancing started once more. The groups danced as before, and soon the Zuni ended their festivities to continue a few days later to the request of Nawehshe from the Zuni village. The people waited only a couple of days before going into Zuni where they agreed to dance in two days.

The same preparations were made as in Nutria. The Bow Priests would all gather and offerings of corn pollen would be given before dancing started. Then the fires were lit to indicate the start of the dance. Then U-ka-yah, Kehlequeh, Coouisi, and Mopahsi, the council for Nutria, gave word to dance the rain dance, this time for the use of a plaza dance place. The men asked for the masked dancers to come to Nutria. The Brain Clan agreed to come in four days after their songs had been finished and when their leader had been chosen.

The man returned and told the villagers, and so the four days passed quickly and soon they came to Nutria. They prepared food and fed dancers, and the dancing commenced. When they finished, they were sent back with the offerings from the people from Nutria. Then quiet settled over the villages until the next dance would be asked for.

Periods of dancing lasted as long as the people were enthusiastic about the dancing. But when they stopped, they also stopped for long periods of time.

8 The Two Orphans and Their Grandmother

A long time ago in Halona famine came over the land, and slowly the village came to be deserted except for one family. The mother and father and two small children stayed, until one day the mother found their food supply extremely low. She exclaimed about their situation to the father and he immediately decided they should leave for the land toward the rising sun, for he had heard of the wealth of many different tribes, but that they should leave the children as they were too heavy and would only slow them down. The mother agreed, so the next day they discreetly prepared what they would take along with them. With the preparations almost finished they realized that dusk had fallen so they made ready the bedding on the floor for the children. When they had been fed and put to bed the children fell asleep almost instantly.

The two started out and trudged on through the night until, toward dawn, they came to a big lake near the Laguna village. There they set their eyes upon the great fields of corn and other crops. They stopped to rest as the morning sun began to shine upon them.

Back in Halona the children stirred in their sleep and awakened shortly. They looked about searchingly for their parents and found no one around. Their first thought was that their parents had perhaps gone to visit someone who might still be around, so the older brother told his little brother not to worry, that they would find them. They left their house and hand in hand started out to look for their mother and father. They checked everywhere in the quiet village but found no one until they were at the outskirts of the village, where they found an old lady sitting alone in her house. "So here we have found you, our grandmother."

"Yes, my poor children, come in. Your parents have left you to go to another settlement where there is an abundance of food available. This is why small children should go to bed early so that they would wake early enough to keep their eyes on their parents. How are you getting along? Do you still have food to eat?"

"Yes, but our cornmeal is quickly diminishing."

"We shall go to your house then and we shall all feed upon the little we have left." The three came to the house and there sparingly ate the cornmeal.

The following day their grandmother said to the boys, "You go to the mountainside where there once grew great fields of corn. You will pick the dried cornstalks and bring them so I will make some Shu-ma-gho-lowa as a blessing to the spirits for our ancestors believed these blessings would be an aid to bring corn pollen to our people so they may plant the seeds and receive the corn upon which our livelihood depends."

Without reply the two brothers went out and gathered as many cornstalks as they could carry and brought them home to their grandmother.

"Here you are, grandmother, would this be enough?"

"Yes, now place them in the basket." When the boys had done this, she continued, "Now you will do this." The grandmother removed the outer layer of the stalk and cut off a piece from each end and placed the stalks toward the four directions. She told the boys to do the same and when they had all done this the grandmother went into another room and brought out the paints that belonged to the priest, the two boys' father.

"You will paint these yellow and the others blue, red, white, one spotted, and the rest black." When all the short rods of stalks had been painted the grandmother sat down and made thin strips like string from the outer coverings. When she had finished, the bundles were tied over the places the boys slept. "Now, if we have done this right perhaps our ancestors will bring the seeds that we need desperately. We are finished so we must go retire."

After eating a few bites of dry cornmeal the three lay down in their respective places and were soon asleep. When all was quiet, to the west there came an opening like a tunnel, leading in so far that there was no end to be seen. At that moment the Shu-ma-gho-lowa began to move, wriggling loose of the strips that bound them together. Soon they had all freed themselves and went into the opening, which brought them to Koh-thlou-wah-la-wah.

When all had come to the sacred place they were asked to stop there, as the spirits of the dead were at their rituals. When the spirits had come to a halt with their activities the leader spoke. "Let all be still as our children have come upon us and we know not who prepared them."

The Shu-ma-gho-lowa were directed to the center of a huge kiva and were addressed, "Now you shall speak, our children. Whoever prepared you did so rightly as you have come into our lives."

"Surely enough," one spoke, continuing, "From Halona we have come for there is nothing there. It is windswept, cold, and desolate. Even when our people have tried their best, planting our seeds, there has come nothing of us. The wind blows everything away and there is no nourishment on which corn can grow. There is no food. The two children who prepared us were left by their parents who had migrated to another land in search of food. We have come to ask if you would give us the blessing with which we can help our people. Will you give us what we ask for?"

"Surely!" the spirits answered. The spirits representing different kernels of corn came forth with great baskets of kernels. These were tightly bundled and given to the Shu-ma-gho-lowa.

"We shall go now. Perhaps you may someday come to see and check on our people." With this the Shu-ma-gho-lowa came back to the house where they once again bound themselves over the sleeping heads of the two young boys. Then each dropped a kernel down upon the floor by the boys' heads. After the first kernels, the Shu-ma-gho-lowa began to drop more kernels, and the boys awoke and awakened their grandmother.

"Grandmother, is it raining?"

"No, there is no rain coming down."

"But we can hear the patter of rain upon our covers."

"Be quiet and wait a little while more, because there is no rain leaking from the roof." Shortly, all around the boys there lay kernels uncountable. Then the Shu-ma-gho-lowa stopped dropping the kernels down, and as soon as it became quiet in the room the boys spoke again.

"There is no more patter, grandmother." The grandmother rose and quickly built a fire in the fireplace. From the light they could see the kernels sprinkled all over the floor.

"Look. The Shu-ma-gho-lowa have brought you kernels. Get up now." The grandmother parched a portion of the corn over the fire and they sat up eating. For the next three nights the Shu-ma-gho-lowa dropped kernels down on the floor, until they had dropped all of them. When they had completely stopped, the grandmother told the boys, "The Shu-ma-gho-lowa did not drop any more kernels last night so now we must go with the rest of the kernels we have left."

With the basket of kernels they left for the fields. Once there the grandmother told the boys, "Now to the north you will send the yellow kernel." The grandmother said some words that the boys were to say as they sent the kernel to its destination. The boys went a few steps to the north and there spoke, "You will go to the north whereupon you will watch over the waters that come to bring us fertile lands and crops." As they let go, the kernels went to the north and were soon out of sight.

The blue was sent to Gyalishshenah, the red to Alahonqueh, to the east the white, and toward the skies the Shu-ma-gho-lowa and the black kernels were sent up. These last two circled over the land before they disappeared. Then the grandmother and the two boys went back into the house.

"You will now sit upon the roof in the sunlight so you may see if there will be anyone who should come upon us," said the grandmother, and the two boys climbed up on the roof. Shortly they spotted smoke rising in the air not far from their house. They informed their grandmother of this and were told, "Wait patiently. Perhaps he will come closer."

They sat up and looked about and shortly more smoke went up and it was closer. They shouted down to their grandmother. She told them to remain on the roof and keep their eyes watching, as the being might come.

Soon the boys saw a small figure coming out of the wooded area, and they saw too that he was very dark and had spots all over his body. They shouted down to their grandmother describing the small figure, and she exclaimed, "It must be our father, the Fire God. Wait!" She ran in and quickly ground some corn into meal and came back out. She told the boys to come in and sit down along the wall. The two boys did so quickly and just as they had sat down, the Fire God came to the door and struck the four sides of the door, opened it, and entered.

"Good afternoon, how have you fared these days?"

"We have been getting along," the grandmother replied, and asked the Fire God to sit upon a large rock slab.

"Our father, the Bowdewa, asked that you be looked after so I have come," he said.

"We have but a few kernels left from the droppings of the Shu-ma-gho-lowa."

"That is why I have come. I have brought you some more food." The Fire God laid down the bundle that he took from his back and unrolled it. There was dried deer meat and piki bread.

"You will keep the piki bread stored in a little bin and the meat hung out in the other room. You shall eat well and plentifully for this will not be depleted."

After he had given them the food the Fire God started to leave; the grandmother and the two boys sprinkled some cornmeal on him and he was on his way.

The grandmother quickly prepared the meat and took out the piki bread and they all ate. Day after day they continued to eat well, as the piki bread multiplied itself and the dried deer meat never reduced in quantity.

When the spring came the Bowdewa sent the Fire God out again to check on the boys and their grandmother and to see where they could help to plant crops for them. The boys were sitting atop their roof eating when they spotted the smoke rising toward the sky. They hurried into the house and informed their grandmother. They were told to wait outside until he came closer before they came inside to wait for him. When the Fire God was not far away the two boys scrambled in and sat waiting for him. He came and made his entrance the same way as before.

"How have you been these past days?"

"Good, sit down," the grandmother answered.

The Fire God inquired of the food supply and again presented the three with a bundle of food. He then took a handful of cornmeal and asked, "Now, where is a field where we can help you plant some crops?"

"By the pathway where your fathers go."

"Very well, we will come in four days and you will wait for us at the fields. We will come as the spirits of natural elements and some as Kachinas to plant the seeds."

Three days passed and on the fourth day they awoke to find the sky hidden by dark clouds. "Go on, they will come soon," the grandmother said, and sent the boys with the basket.

In the fields the boys prepared places where the leaders were to sit. Then came the beings and the spirits, as rain sprinkled upon the ground. When the Kachinas came upon them, the boys asked them to sit in a row, the Bowdewa first, Yamoohukdo, Sayatashsah, another Yamoohukdo, then the Fire God. Behind them, the Hahdashogho was asked to plant the kernels of corn in the field. With the corn, replicas of small game—rabbits, groundhogs, squirrels—and deer were placed in the ground. When they had finished, the boys were told, "We have planted everything for you. Now all you have to do is check on these every so often."

"Let us go up to the house then, grandmother is waiting for us." The boys led the way with the Kachinas following. When they got to the house the grandmother gave them offerings of food bundles. With the Yamoohukdo ahead, the Kachinas left, and rain began to fall.

The following day the boys went to the field to check on the crops and found leaves and flowers of crops blossoming, while the ears of rabbits, deer, groundhogs, and squirrels protruded from the ground. A short while later the animals began to rise up and were soon completely free from the soil, and the corncobs grew large kernels upon them.

The Bowdewa asked once more to have the three checked

and again the Fire God came and asked if the food was holding out and if they had checked the field to see if anything was growing. The boys told him all they had seen and they were told to pick the corn crop so that their grandmother could boil the corn. The next day they went to the field and picked the cobs of corn and ripened melons so their grandmother could boil and prepare the food.

Then came time to bring home the deer, which had grown rapidly. The Fire God came to see the progress of the animals. The deer were shown to him and he replied that the next day the Kachinas would come again to help with the game hunting. He left again after he had been sprinkled with cornmeal. Upon his return the Bowdewa asked how the crops had progressed and was told that the Fire God would bring the Hahdashogho with him to take care of the animals. And so it was arranged.

The next day the boys went to the fields and sat waiting for the Kachinas. When they appeared they immediately started on the harvesting of some of the crops and the killing of the game. All this was done by sundown and the Kachinas departed again.

The mother and father decided to go back to their children to see if conditions had improved. The father came to check on the situation and found the boys eating well and eyed the stores of melons and cornmeal. He greeted his children and came to embrace them. The children ran from him and went to stand by their grandmother. The father looked at them for a short time, then sat to eat a melon that lay on the table. He finished the melon and spoke again, but there was no response, so he picked up a melon and went out and started back to his wife to tell her of the wealth of their children.

The wife immediately bundled together a light load of their

belongings and they came, spending the night out in the woods. The following evening they came within sight of their house and saw that sparks were coming down from the chimney. They hurried down and entered into the house. They were greeted and the mother tried to embrace her children and her mother, but the three fled out of the house. The mother and father decided not to bother with them and began to feast upon the foods brought to the house by the Kachinas and the supernatural beings.

The three fled out of the house and hid in a darkened corner through the night. When the morning came the grandmother and her grandchildren lay dead, as their spirits came to be at Koh-thlou-wah-la-wah.

Because of this our grandfathers believe the Kachinas and the two abandoned children with their grandmother have helped to bring the abundance of food and material wealth now enjoyed by our people today.

9 Zuni and Their Ways of Living

In the days of our grandparents, the tribes sometimes brought onto themselves troubles and hard times. The Hopi were attacked by the Zuni. When the Zuni reached the First Mesa, the Hopi fled to the second, while the Zuni took the livestock from the First Mesa. Then one of the Hopi brought much horror and a great loss of lives to the Zuni.

The people who were to be our friends fought one another

and ideas of counterattacks were disposed of, when the people who would be involved in those battles were taken into consideration. Then the culture and traditions would be stripped of any significance, if the battles persisted and the possibility of killing off each other was pondered.

The Hopi were not willing to risk what their forefathers brought upon the lands and therefore dispensed of any avenging battles. But even as one group relented, or if another did not want to fight, there were always some persistent in their ways of aggression. But for the time, not many of the renegades valued their ways of keeping peace among the many people.

If one person had the smallest grievance or grudge against a person, the lives of many lost were accounted to gain one's satisfaction. Such were in battles, that if a man wished harm on a single enemy, he would approach the opposing side and plan a massacre of his own people, for the satisfaction of avenging the wrong done against him.

"Sebuloutche" was the term for the people who had turned against their own kind.

But through the same means, the warring tribes fared well, surviving their cruelness toward one another. If, for instance, the Navajo wanted to raid Zuni, if there was a chance that among the Navajo there was a friend of the Zuni, he would come down as an informant, warning the people and making arrangements to attack their attackers.

If one should capture a person, the bartering of valuables in exchange for the person would commute and exchanges would secure peace for a short time.

As long as the battling tribes kept fighting there would be a famine, and great periods of starvation and need. The necessities of life became hard to come by. As if by some power, the natural elements, wind, the hot scorching sun, would beat upon the earth, making it impossible for the few who tried to grow crops and tried to produce anything to help themselves. What few things were stored away for hard times would be depleted and the Zuni would roam about into the other tribal settlements, where they would work for the food they ate.

Today, it is totally different. We need not worry about what to feed ourselves. We depend on the food provided us by the white men. Our children do not eat what their grandparents before ate. If there is as much as a hint of Indian food on their tables daily, the white man's food is preferred. We do not work hard for what we attain these days. We live without the constant struggle for survival.

Our grandparents were lucky if they had a few grains of corn that could be roasted or ground into little patties, making them last as long as possible. Maybe it is because of the grandparents before our grandparents, who brought onto this land the ways of living and their thoughts of how their children should live, that the pattern in which we exist today is toilless and peaceful. Should all our Zuni ways have been lost, our people today might not be as secure as they are.

With the ways of the white man entering into our lives, perhaps it will not be long before our people become a wandering tribe, aimlessly roving the path of self-deterioration and destruction. But it is for our children to decide and work for. We cannot tell them of the way our people survived, for they would not believe us. We must just hope they, too, can survive what lies before them.

Unkestine, Storyteller

Weekooty Iule, Storyteller

Oscar Gaspar, Storyteller

Henry Natewa, Storyteller and Former Governor

Nastacio, Storyteller, Medicine Man, and Former Governor

(Left to Right) Harry Paquin, Storyteller; Albert Hallion, Storyteller and Rain Priest; Kucate, Storyteller; Lonkeena, Storyteller and Historian; Acque, Storyteller; James Kanteena, Storyteller, Rain Priest, and Medicine Man

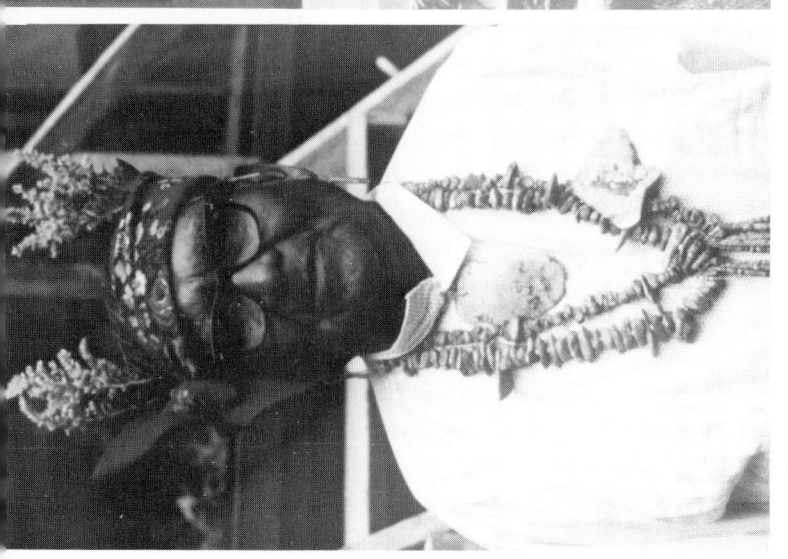

Tom Awelagte, Storyteller and Medicine Man

Owelion, Storyteller and Priest of the Bow

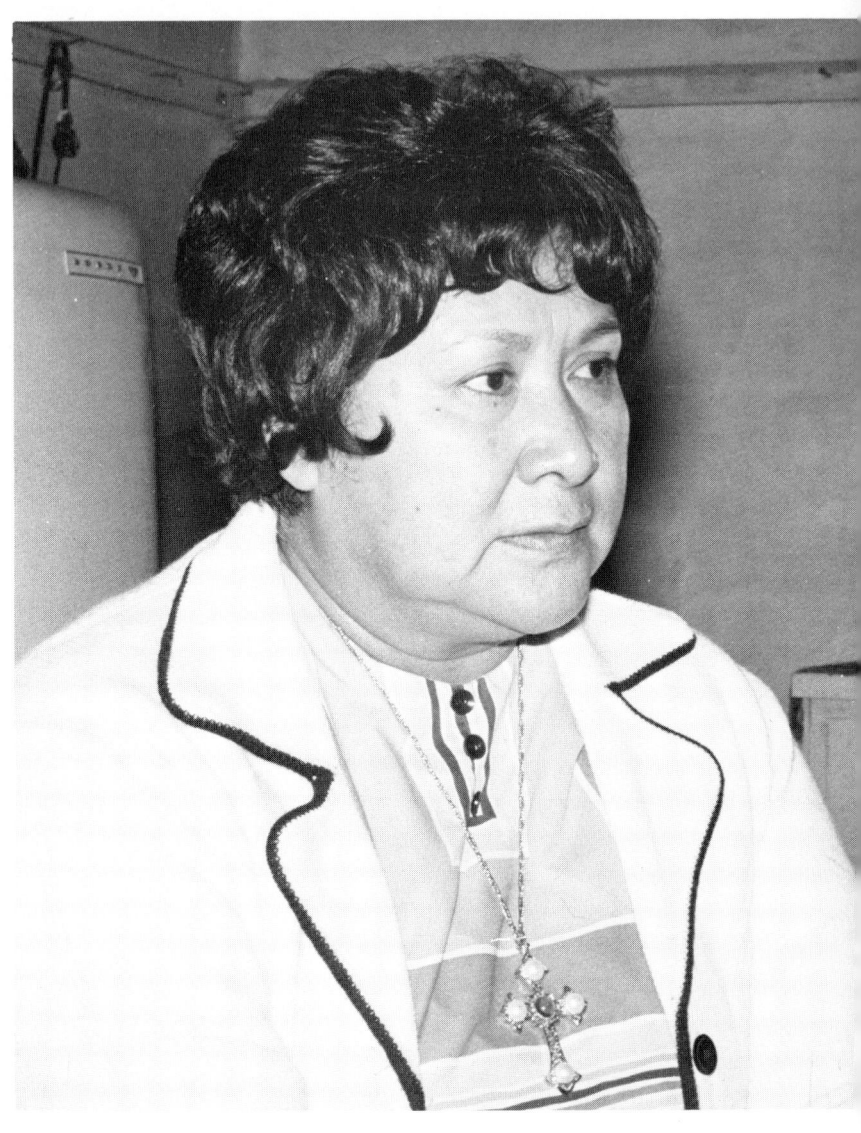

Virginia Lewis, Editor and Wife of Governor Robert E. Lewis

II HISTORY

10 Poorest Days of Enote

*A legend told by Enote and
translated by Alvina Quam*

For as long as I can remember, we have been struggling for survival. With barely any food, we grew up hungry. Although we had a few sheep, we could not eat them unless we were sure that the young lambs could survive the shortage of food and live to bear a few more head.

At times, ground cornmeal made into tortillas was all we had to live on. It was like rationing food. If the tortillas happened to burn, we had to eat them just the same.

And clothes, we were lucky to have what we had on. There were only a few traders who traded with the Indians. When we could afford to buy cloth our clothes would then be made.

Our crops, what few seeds we had, would be planted only to be burned up by the droughts. There were never enough rainstorms and the water from the rivers would soon become exhausted. Dried-up river beds would be all that was left. Once in a while, when there was enough food, we made it last. If we happened to be herding sheep, only a bag of cornmeal and chile would be our food supply.

When spring came, lambs were born, and soon after the sheep would be shorn. During those days people depended on one another to help shear the sheep. There were no such things as shears or cutting implements available. Anything with a sharp edge sufficed. Thus it took a long time to shear even a small herd of sheep.

When autumn came, if one prolonged the harvest of crops, the cold weather would set in and frost would kill the crops. Oftentimes locust was our food supply. When the cold air started to drive the locusts into their hibernating places, we would take hoes, poles, and containers and go after them in their burrows, taking them and putting them in our containers. We would take the locusts home and soak them overnight in the water. When they had been soaked, they would be put in a pot and placed over an open fire. Then they would be roasted until toasty brown. Put a little salt on them and they were a delicacy. The locusts may have looked terrible, but after eating them the appearance no longer mattered. Rarely did we have breakfast or an afternoon meal. When supper came we ate as much as we could afford.

We never dreamed Zuni would ever be as prosperous as it has become. Our children no longer have to work their bones off to fight for survival.

Yes, we were very poor when we were young, but all the work we put into our lives made it more enjoyable, and to think our efforts to keep the Zuni people together had not been a total waste.

11 The Return of the Zuni Slave Woman

To the west of the plaza, now in the center of the village, a young Zuni maiden went down to the spring for some water.

While there by herself, she was captured by a party of Navajos coming from Wemyahwa. She was taken to the Blue Mountains northwest of Zuni. Blindfolded with the belt of her dress, she was seated on top of a horse and led to a place unknown to her.

When they reached their destination the Navajos took her blindfold off and she was shown to her captors. Then another Zuni woman, captive of the Navajos, was sent for to interpret what was said between the Navajos and the Zuni maiden. One captor of the maiden informed the interpreter, "I have brought this girl here and she now lives with me. She will go out with her sisters [Navajo women] to herd sheep and they will speak for her their language, and teach her their words. She must not be alarmed for we will not harm her. For us, the Navajos, to mistreat a captive is forbidden."

The interpreter related to the captive the words of her master. "You must not worry. Do not think of your home or relations as this will only be depressing. You will be well taken care of."

"No, I will not worry. I must have been destined to my present predicament."

They lived with the girl, teaching her the Navajo language, weaving, and other skills required to be a good wife. As the years passed, the Navajos from a far different settlement grew hostile to the young Zuni maiden. No one knew the reason for their hostility. Jealousy was thought to be the only basis for such a hate as theirs. To assure the captive's safety, the captor announced that only a union between them could stop the growing hostility, so they were married. The young girl did not think it was right, as she was a captive, to work for her captor. Also, she had grown to like the man as a parent.

The hostility quieted a little and their lives were back to normal, but only for a short time. Almost three years had gone by and the Zuni woman bore two sons for her husband. As their sons grew older and played about, the Navajos grew discontented again. Jealousy turned to intense hate and they came ready to dispose of the Zuni woman and her two sons. After two more years had gone by, the Navajos had decided to dispose of the woman and her children. The husband became annoyed and finally relented, turning his wife and two children to the Navajos.

He built a nice home for them to live in. He worked on the house until he thought it was built the way it should be. Then he told his wife, "We will separate now. My people do not like our union and so it would be best if we parted and kept peace among the people. I will give you a share of the sheep with which you will feed my two sons. You will be well taken care of."

They were moved to their house and set up comfortably and he left. The same night the Navajos went to the husband and asked if he had relented and done as they wished. He informed them that although it was forbidden for them to harm their captives in any way, he could do nothing to stop them. He told them, "They live by themselves in a house I built for them. You will find them home."

It was agreed then that the woman and her two children would be killed in four days on the fourth morning. But among the Navajos there was a man who did not want the woman and her children to die. He came only to watch and see what would happen.

The days would quickly pass and soon the four days would be up. That night when the rest of the Navajos went home, the man who didn't want the woman and her children to be killed rode up to his home but stood only a short moment, then turned around, going back to the house where the three lived. He left his horse tied to a tree some distance from their house. He walked to the house and entered, for they were not yet in bed. He was invited to sit and as he did he asked, "So you live here now, do you?"

"Yes, we moved only a few days ago after the house had been built and given to us."

"That is only because your days left to live here have already been numbered. Four days from now you are all to die. That is why you were given this house and whatever else you were given. But I do not want you to die, so I have come."

The woman suddenly understood why there had been so many nice things given to them. She exclaimed, "Alas! So that is why we were given the house and the sheep."

"Yes, that is the only reason they gave you the things. So you would not think or worry about anything. For only a few days you would possess the things you were given, but they will all be taken back."

"But what can we do? We cannot fight those Navajos alone."

"Four days from now, at night, you go south of your house behind the small hill. There I will wait for you."

"If you think that is right, we will do it."

"Yes, that is the only way you can survive what is planned for you. Tomorrow, or the next day, you will kill a sheep and fix yourself food to take on a journey. Prepare your belongings in bundles, ready to take. Take along a jug of water to drink. When you start out, go to your husband's house and circle his house once and proceed to the hill. You will first go through your herd of sheep. You must walk a short distance from each other. Do not all walk together. Come behind the hill and I will be waiting for you."

The man left, with this information sinking into the depths of the woman's mind. They went to bed, but she could not sleep thinking of how anybody could be so cruel: thinking of the irony of how nicely they were taken care of so they would not think of, or worry about, what was to happen to them.

The woman stayed awake all night. Early the next morning, the two boys took care of their sheep until noon, then they went to their house to eat. After they had eaten their mother told them, "Children, you will bring one of the sheep here so we can kill it and make ready our food supplies." The two boys did not question their mother and brought home a sheep. They had no knowledge of how to slaughter a sheep but their mother did. Quickly she killed the sheep and skinned it. Then she quartered it, making slabs of meat from the tender parts of the animal. She hung the meat out on tree branches to dry into jerky. By that time dusk had fallen and they went to bed.

On the fourth night they gathered as much wood as the house would hold. They they took their belongings and their food packs. They put plenty of wood in the fireplace to keep the fire burning, for appearances. Then they gave out their packs and put them on their backs and started out for the husband's house. They circled the house as they had been instructed to do and went on until they reached their herd of sheep. Walking a distance away from one another, they made their way through the herd, going south. Each of them walked toward the hill until they met; then, going a little bit farther, they saw the man waiting for them. As they came closer he spoke to them.

"My children, I will help you tonight. I might be able to save you. Tomorrow the Navajos will come to kill you. They will go to your house first. Finding you gone they will be sure to come looking for you. Tonight, I will try to take you out of here. Go to your land in Zuni. I know where it is and how to get there. In the south there is a mesa, and above it, when night falls, a bright star shines, but only for a short time. When it reaches the short distance it disappears back where it came out. You will follow this star because it is right above the Zuni village. Tonight, you will start out and will continue until dawn comes. You will stop during the day and find a place to hide. Make sure it is concealed from open view. There you will stay all day. Do not show yourselves. When dusk falls again, you will then go out, going as fast as you can. You may be sure that they will look thoroughly for you. They will follow your tracks closely, so take care."

"We will do as you say."

"Just make sure you stay with the star, because it is right above your village." With those last words of encouragement, the three started out directly to the south. They walked without rest for many miles. Through the night they did not give thought to anything else except reaching safety and refuge. As dawn slowly came, they reached one of the many small cliffs in the area. They ascended to the top of the cliff and made sure to conceal themselves from view. The mother wanted to find still a better place to hide, so she said to her two sons, "You will stay here. I am going down to find another place to hide."

She went a little way down the cliff, walking along a narrow log; then found another opening, barely visible, also covered with brush. She proceeded to uncover the opening and found it to be a cave big enough to hide the three of them adequately.

After she cleared the cave of debris she went back up to fetch her two sons. "Come, my children, we will go down."

The two boys gathered their packs and followed their mother. They went into the cave, the two boys first, then their packs, and lastly their mother, who had to conceal their tracks and close the opening with the brush and tree branches.

In the meantime, to their home there came a group of Navajos, men ready to kill them. As they approached the house there was no sign of life. It was quiet and still. A man was sent to the house to check on them. He went to the house and found it empty. In the fireplace the ashes from the fire of the night before had grown cold.

He quickly informed the rest of the men, and they instantly agreed that they must go after them. First, they dismounted from their horses and looked for any trace of footprints or tracks. After they found them they followed the tracks until they came to the small hill south of their home. There they found horse tracks coming from the east.

"Alas! There must have been someone here who helped them flee. They could not have known which way to go. They are not familiar with this land. If we find that person who helped them escape, we will kill him, too."

They followed the trail until they came to the cliff. There the tracks disappeared. No more tracks could be found. The south side was thoroughly checked for tracks, but none was found. The Navajo called out the woman's name, and she heard them, but gave no response. No tracks could be found because they had walked along a ledge of limestone, making sure they did not step in the loose sand. The Navajo men finally gave up their search and left.

The three stayed in the cave, not a sound could be heard from them. They stayed until they could barely see any light. Then the mother came out from the cave. Very carefully she looked out, cautious with her every move. She stood there for a while, she was listening intently for any human sounds. After she stood out there for a while, she was sure that no one was around, so she called for her sons to get ready because they were going to leave shortly.

The two little boys were afraid of the possibility of the Navajos waiting for them to show themselves. The mother finally coaxed them to come out and they assumed the fast pace down the cliff. They walked all night until almost dawn when they reached a small hill and stopped for a short while. By that time the boys were tired and complaining about their feet hurting. As soon as the sun came up along the horizon they started walking again, after resting just long enough to let the aching and burning in their feet lessen.

"Now let us go, my children, you must assert your whole being and all your strength for the next few miles. We have come onto our land. The two buttes ahead are a part of the Zuni land. A short distance south from those buttes is where we shall live. We have come now. We would go through the little gulch between the buttes and Zuni, but the Navajos might possibly be scouting around there and they might see us and we would be killed. I don't think it would be a very good idea for us to go this way. Toward the west we well might go and then come directly from the west into Zuni."

They again put their packs upon their backs and headed west. As they reached the little mountain named Saddle Ridge, they headed back east for the Zuni village.

They came upon a field where two men worked tending their corn crop. The men looked, and saw what they thought to be a Navajo woman, with her two sons. The woman indeed looked totally Navajo with her big bun of hair and her long skirt, the costume of the Navajo. She came forth and spoke to the two men in halting Zuni, which had not been spoken for so long. The two men still thought they were Navajo and so one of them instructed the other to go into the village and tell their Bow Priest of the people they thought were Navajos. He told his partner, "The Bow Priests will gather the people and tell them of these people, then they will decide what to do. They might want to kill them. While you are gone, I will give them corn to roast and eat, also watermelon, then they will be well fed."

The woman and her two sons were fed and the other man told the Bow Priest about the woman, then they in turn told their people. All the people agreed on killing them.

The man who had stayed with the three questioned the woman thoroughly. "Are you a Navajo?"

The woman shook her head and answered "No."

Then she spoke her father's name and the man announced, "Alas! You must be the one they captured many years ago. Indeed there is a man in the village who has a daughter missing."

About that time the other man came back and told of the people coming, and again he was sent back. "Go back and tell them that this is the maiden who disappeared many years ago. She had been made a slave first and then she married her captor. These are the two sons she bore for her husband."

The man left again. He met the group of Zunis only a short distance from the field. He spoke to the head Bow Priest. "I have come to inform you that the woman and her children are not Navajos. She is the missing daughter of one of the elders in the village. She was a captive of the Navajos."

The group proceeded to turn back to their village, when the man asked, "Is there any one in the group who belongs to the Clown Clan?"

"Yes, there are two here that belong to that clan."

The man went on to the field with the two men from the

Clown Clan and of the two men, one named Yepsheyeh questioned the girl in Navajo. The girl once more told of her captivity and how she was married to her captor so she wouldn't be killed. After two years, she told them, she had given birth to two sons, but still they were wanted so they could be killed; after so much pressure against her husband he finally relented and did as the Navajos wished him to do. She told how he built them a house and gave them sheep and a share of his possessions to make them think nothing of their separation. Then she told of the man who helped them escape their death. She told of how he instructed them to follow the star shining brightly above the village of Zuni. Without the aid of that man they could not have escaped.

After hearing out her story of captivity the clan members then consecrated her and the two boys with prayers. The three were brought to the village into their father's house. After the clan members had consecrated them, they were to be initiated into the Clown Clan, but the boys objected and so their mother alone was initiated.

The two boys were given names by the clan, Thlabeyakya and Tsadiyashinne.

The three were accepted into the village with the warm welcome and were made to feel at home.

12   The Navajo and She-She's Wife

Many years ago, when our village was situated in a tight cluster and when the houses were atop one another along the south

edge, there lived a man named She-She. A little way to the
north, where the big plaza is now, the woman who was married
to She-She lived. When they got married the woman moved
in with her in-laws. In that same house, in another room, a
group of Navajos met each night.

During the day the lady would fix two bowls of blue corn
meal to make piki bread with. She would fix them and put
them away in her bread bins, expecting to find them in the
morning. But each morning she found the bread bins empty.
For many days she did not mention the peculiarity, but
wondered much about it.

Spring came and she had become tired of making all the
piki bread only to find them gone each morning. Once again
she prepared the piki bread, and when it was time to go to
bed she took her blankets to the rooftop where she lay down
by the entrance. She lay with her face down, looking into
the room below. From another room the Navajos began to
fill the room. Shortly, they sat about and the meeting started.
For a long time the men talked and the woman wondered
what they talked about. She thought perhaps it was about
someone they wanted to hurt or destroy. The meeting lasted
until late into the night. At last, as the Navajos stood up
to leave, the lady's husband brought out the piki bread and gave
one to each of the Navajo.

The woman, knowing what happened to the piki bread
now, wondered what the purpose of their visits was. She went
off to sleep thinking about what possible reasons there were for
the Navajos' visit. The next morning she woke up and once
more started to fix the batter for the piki bread. When she
had fixed one bowl she decided she would not fix another, for
she was not making the bread for the Navajos.

Her husband, knowing that she had found out about their

meetings, went to the Wide Wall kiva where he casually asked about the dancing the clan was planning to do, with the intention of premeditating a scheme upon his wife's life.

"We do not know when we shall dance. There have not been very many men present at the meetings. Why? Do you wish to join our dancing group?"

"No, it is nothing like that. I just want to know when you will start dancing," he asked.

"We will gather tonight and will probably decide on the commencing date."

"If you should, I wish to know the date you set."

"We shall notify you if we decide tonight," replied the head of the clan. That night as the leaders gathered, the question was put forth to them and one replied, "We are almost ready. There have been enough men present to dance, so we shall set the date tonight. I think four days from now would be agreeable."

So it was agreed and She-She was told the commencing date of the dance. Once more the lady prepared a batter for the piki bread, thinking to herself, "I will not make the blue piki bread today, for I am sure the Navajos will come again. Instead I will make the red corn meal. They do not particularly like that kind." So she fixed one bowl of batter for the piki bread. That same night the Navajos once more gathered and the wife lay upon the roof, looking into the room where the talking commenced once again.

Down by the river where the Navajos had left their horses with the reins tied to the willows, a man had also noticed them coming and going. That night he knew that the Navajos would not leave until very late. He came and took the beautiful handwoven saddle blankets that he had admired for some time. He wrapped them in a nice neat bundle and ran home.

The night had gone swiftly and as the hours approached dawn, the Navajos adjourned the meeting to go home. Before they departed, She-She spoke to them, "Four days from now, there will be dancing. On that day, early morning, we will eat and then I shall ask my wife to go pick some fruit at Hehshokdahque. She will go and you will be there waiting for her, to take her."

"If that is what you want, yes, that will be done," replied the Navajo.

Because the wife had discovered the meetings, She-She had placed her life in the hands of the Navajo. So three days passed and early on the fourth morning, as the two sat eating, She-She spoke to his wife.

"After we have eaten, go to the peach orchard and pick some fruit. There might come some Mudheads and it is embarrassing when there is nothing to give them." To his surprise she got mad and retorted, "I will go when I please. I know what I have to do. Why are you telling me?"

Before she bit into the rolled piki bread she threw it down and picked another piece, folded it, and placed it in her basket. Placing the basket upon her back, she started out. She went half the distance to the orchard and she began thinking that it was too dangerous for anyone to go out alone, so she decided to go back and ask her brother or sister if one of them would come along. She turned back to the village and came to her parents' house. They were eating when she entered and she was invited to sit and eat with them.

"I have come to ask my sister if she would accompany me to the orchard to pick some fruit."

"Of course, I will go." The girl also took a piece of piki bread, folded it, and placed it in her basket. Then she put the basket upon her back and they started out. Soon they came down where one of their brothers lived, but their brother already had left for his parents' house. When he reached their house he immediately noticed the absence of his sister.

"Where is my sister today?"

"She went with her sister to Hehshokdahque to pick some fruit. Her sister did not want to go alone so she asked if your sister would accompany her. They left a short while ago."

"Alas! Why did the two of them go? They know it is dangerous to go out even with companions, especially for women. I will go out after them." The lad left, ran up to his home, took down his bow and arrows, and ran after the two sisters. He caught up with them just before they reached the orchard. The girls greeted him. "You have come now."

"Yes," replied the lad, breathing hard, "I have come because you should not walk out here by yourselves. It is dangerous for anyone to come out."

The Navajos had started out the night before, spending the night at the White Clay Lake, then coming on the next morning. She-She's wife told her brother and sister about her husband. "That ugly, terrible man will surely follow us. If he should catch up with us do not speak to him at all."

Soon they came and sure enough the husband was coming up from behind them, asking, "Is this all the farther you have come?" The two women did not reply but their brother answered, "Yes, indeed. It is a slow process for women to cover much distances. This is all we have come." As the husband made small talk neither of the women responded but their brother continued to reply to the man's conversation.

By then they had come into the orchard where She-She's wife sat under the shade to rest a bit. Her sister spoke, "Well, well. I will go in a little bit farther where our peach orchard is. I will be back shortly."

The other sister quickly protested, "No, that is not necessary. Do not go any farther. We will both fill our baskets here without any trouble. Then we will start back home again."

"Very well, that is fine. It is quite a way into the orchard where our trees are."

So they started picking the ripened peaches and soon their baskets were filled. They wrapped some in their aprons and were ready to start home. Their brother had gone on into the Saddle Forest while the husband remained near his wife's orchard, a short distance to the north. He was walking along the cliff of a mountain. She-She's wife said, "Maybe I should pick some more so we can eat before we start back home."

"Go ahead and pick some more if you want." She sat down and waited while She-She's wife went farther in the orchard for better peaches, which she wrapped in her apron, and came back. They had begun to unwrap their food, when suddenly they were ambushed by some Navajos. She-She's wife was so frightened that she ran back into the orchard, where the Navajos all came upon her. When they had her captive they rode on toward home, while her sister ran west, jumping into a gully and hiding herself.

She-She's wife was blindfolded and strapped to a horse, then led away. The sister, well hidden, listened until there were no more sounds. Meanwhile, their brother came back from his little excursion to find them gone. He saw the baskets sitting full on the ground, but his sisters were nowhere in sight. He called out to them several times before his sister answered from her hiding place. The lad walked over and found his sister sitting in a little niche behind a bush along the bank of the gully.

"Why are you sitting in there?"

"Because my sister has been captured and taken by the

Navajos. We were just getting ready to eat when they ambushed us. She was so frightened that she ran back into the orchard. I jumped into this gully."

"It has happened. This is why I told you it was dangerous for you to come out here. But what can we do? I am alone and her husband probably won't come with me. I am afraid there is nothing we can do. He probably asked the Navajos to do this horrible thing. It is their fault for they did not want each other."

So the two returned home with the peaches. As they came upon some mounds the husband came along and casually asked where his wife was. For a long time neither replied, but as She-She continued his questioning the brother finally spoke.

"Where do you think she is? You ought to know, because you asked your Navajo friends to come after her and they did. Why did you have them come here in the first place? I am not happy. I do not want to speak to you again!"

With that the brother and sister walked on, ignoring She-She as he kept talking, trying to get the two to speak to him. Just because his wife had found out about his meetings with the Navajo he had turned her over to them.

Then was a time for hatred and vengeance for any and all crimes.

13 Raid before Coming of the Shalako

Each year in the winter months the Zunis observed a ceremony, signified as a blessing ritual for new homes. The six kivas of the village each had one Shalako, a god that the Zunis believed to have powers of bestowing a good life. The leaders of each kiva gave out prayersticks every winter to a family assuming the responsibility of building a house to house the Shalako when the final ceremonial rituals were to take place.

Many, many years ago, around autumn, the men of Zuni went out on a raiding party. They went to raid the Navajo settlements, raiding them of their livestock and crops. It took a large amount of food to feed the people during Shalako, and the Zunis did not have their own means of supplying food for their people, so they often raided nearby settlements.

On this particular raiding party it was to be only a short time before the Shalako came to the village. The participating people had gone with the raiding party and they had no idea how long they would be gone. They went north, not knowing when they would return. As they went further into the mountains and entered a gorge, they found a settlement, Navajos by the mass. The Zunis went up the surrounding mountains and overlooked the entire Navajo settlement. When they had gotten themselves organized and settled, the Bow Priest in the raiding party went scouting around the settlement.

"We must pray now."

They gathered in a tight group and chanted their prayers for the war party. The sun had gone down while they prayed. They had no awareness of time until they finished their prayers at the break of dawn. They rose up with a war cry and attacked the Navajos. As the Navajos panicked, alarmed at the sudden attack, they had no defense against the raiding party. The female population of the settlement ran further back into a gorge where they thought they would be safe, while the men rushed around gathering their weapons and getting ready to fight.

As soon as the sun came out, fighting broke out. It lasted all day without food or drink. The Navajos were not pushed back. Their strength was equal to the Zunis and they fought until the Zunis lost ground. The Zunis were pushed into a gorge, and they said among themselves, "Let us not go backwards. Head out toward the open area so we won't be cornered."

The fighting continued without either party letting up or yielding. During the fight, one of the Zuni men was killed and they guarded the body, keeping the Navajos from taking it. Then the Zunis killed a Navajo and that body was also guarded. The fighting came to a slower pace as the sun disappeared into the horizon, and soon the fighting stopped.

The priests gathered and asked, "Where is the body of our dead one?"

"He is still lying upon the ground where he fell," replied one of the men.

"Go get him and we will talk of what to do next."

The men went to get the corpse. They brought it back to the gathering.

"What shall we do now? Shall we stay another day to fight?" asked the man.

"Alas! For what purpose? Our corpse will hinder our fighting strength. It will be of no useful purpose to keep fighting. We will break camp now and go back home. We will not fight anymore unless they come after us and attack us. Then we will fight. If we stay here, we will not do right."

"If that is what you people think, it shall be done. But how are we going to take the corpse back?"

"We will make a stretcher with the poles of the small trees. Four men should be able to carry him without too much trouble."

They immediately set about making the stretcher. They cut two long poles and placed small pieces of wood in the center, tying them together with the ropes they had. When they had finished, they laid a saddle blanket and then placed the corpse on the stretcher. With two men holding the foot, they proceeded toward home. All night they went slowly without stopping for rest. Dawn came and they still had not reached Zuni.

The Navajos had sent out their scouts during the night to check on the Zunis but they came to find the Zunis gone. They started out after them immediately, arguing among themselves as to whether they should go after them and fight or let them go home.

"No, let us not go any farther. We will not do right by vengeance. Let them go. If we follow them, we will be doing wrong. A few of you will ride on after them. When you catch up with them, you will tell them you want no more fighting and you will be friendly to them, and tell them also that someday there will be no need to fight."

A group of men were sent out after the Zunis. These men were all opposed to fighting the Zunis. They rode their horses swiftly, gaining distance rapidly. While the Zunis traveled slowly because of their corpse, the Navajos rode until they sighted the Zunis. They rode rapidly, raising clouds of dust behind them.

The Zunis immediately noticed the dust and exclaimed, "Look, they are coming as we said they would! Take the corpse and go on ahead. If we are lucky, they won't be here until you have gone a little way farther. We will fight. If we can't beat them, they might push us back, so go on, we should catch up with you shortly."

The carriers were replaced and a new team of men took the stretcher and started out again with a faster pace. The men staying behind started to get their weapons ready for fighting. The Navajos came down until they were in full view of the Zunis. They slowed down and approached the Zunis with their hands up in the air as a sign of peace.

A Zuni man shouted, "Look, they do not want to fight. They want peace. Wait! Put down your weapons on the ground and stand still. Do not start anything. We might do a lot of unjust harm. But if they are fooling us, we will be ready for them."

The Navajos had come to a halt and the spokesman for the Zuni men said, "You have come now."

"Yes, we have finally reached you. We did not know how far you had come until we came upon you," said the Navajo.

"Yes, well, we have come a long way."

"Our friends, we have come not to fight. We came to tell you we do not wish any harm or injury. We talked among ourselves and agreed not to fight. We also hope there will be peace among our people some day. If we should ever come to your land, we hope there will be no reason for you to fight us. We had thought how there should be friendship among us, so we do not feel alienated when or if we ever come upon your people."

"Yes, that is the way it should be. We have great happenings and if you ever want to come see us, you should be welcome," said the Zuni men to the Navajos after agreement.

"Yes, we talked much about these things before we came. Our

friends, we have come to bid you farewell and a peaceful ride home. We will have a pact for our friendship."

"That shall be. Come down off your horses."

The Navajo warriors came down off their horses and everybody shook hands, hugging each other and joking, laughing, happy that they had no more fear and distrust for each other.

"Now, our friends, you will have no fear of our people ever attacking you. You will go now, without fear or distrust. We shall go, too. We have agreed upon peace. Have no fear of anyone following you."

The Zunis came toward home. Having completely forgotten about their Shalako ceremony and when it was to be, they thought nothing of coming slowly, taking their time. They proceeded slowly, the carriers of the corpse being replaced every once in a while.

As they came down the mountains, they came into the village of Laguna, and one of the Zunis went to see a friend living there. He took the whole raiding party to the village and there they were fed. After they had eaten, they proceeded to their camp and started talking about what was happening in Zuni.

"Alas! What can be done? Our ceremonial day is only a few days off. Maybe the people will carry it out, regardless of whether we are there. But none of us knows exactly when it is to be. I wonder what is happening," said one man. "We have also the body we have to take back, which is slowing our pace. Couldn't we go back to the village where we ate and ask if we can bury the body there so we can cover the distance to Zuni sooner? If they let us, we should hurry back and see what is happening. We have to see if the Shalakos have come. Or maybe it is the time for them to fast. Or maybe the Mudheads have come already.

We don't know what has been going on. Let us go back and ask."

Two days had passed after the Long Horn preceded the Shalako ceremonies, and the men in the raiding party went back into the village of Laguna. When they gathered the leaders of the village, the Zunis said, "We have come to ask what we should do. It is now time for our big feast. We do not know if the Shalakos have come yet or if the people are waiting till we get back to Zuni before they have the ceremonies. We have the body of one of our men and it has detained us, keeping us from reaching our village sooner. We thought if you consented to our burying the body here, we could keep going without any further delay. We want to see what has happened. Maybe the Shalakos are coming now. We have some men here who are participants in the ritual and they want to get back as fast as they can. What would you advise us to do?"

"Well, since you have a great responsibility at home and you have asked us, we have nothing against letting you bury the body here. Go ahead and bury it tomorrow morning and then hurry on your way to Zuni."

"Then it shall be." The Zuni men left after the Laguna priests had consented to their request. They went back to their camp and slept under the stars.

The next morning, early, the men dug a grave and buried the corpse with a small prayer. They started out for Zuni as soon as they had completed the burial.

The people in Zuni waited two days after the coming of the Long Horn and two more days remained before the coming of the Shalakos. One of the Head Priests exclaimed, "Alas! Our men who went out on the raiding party have not come yet and our big feast day is almost here. What shall be done? Couldn't we postpone it?"

"We don't know. It depends on the six kivas. We will have to gather the leaders of each kiva before we can do anything."

So the kiva leaders held a conclave and talked.

"What is the reason we have met? What do you want to talk about?"

"It is about our men who have gone on a raiding party and have not returned yet. With our big ceremony and feast only two days off, and with some of the participants in the raiding party, we wonder if we could not possibly delay the ceremony for at least two days? If after the two-day delay the men still have not come, the ceremonies will be carried out. They should be here within a few days."

"That could be done. There is nothing wrong with that, so it shall be."

One of the kiva leaders turned to another and asked, "What do you think about that? Do you agree to our thoughts?"

"Yes, I have nothing to say against them. Let us go ahead with the two-day delay. They might be here tomorrow or the next. Everything is ready for the ceremonies so there is no problem. If they do not come in the next two days, we shall go on with the ceremonies."

The kiva leaders and the priests agreed on the delay and so the Shalako ceremonies were postponed for two days.

The day after the agreement for the delay, as the sun was setting, the men came into the village. With a flurry of excitement and people rushing around, they were settled with their affairs in time for the Shalako ceremonies when the postponement came to an end.

As far back as is known, this postponement of the ceremonies has been the only one ever carried through.

14 Spirit World of the Zunis

*Enote's trip to Koh-thlou-wah-la-wah,
as translated by Alvina Quam*

Many years ago, when I was still a young lad, I was taken to the place of our ancestors' dwellings. About twenty-six miles west of Zuni there stands a lone hill amidst the quiet solitude of rolling plains. It took us a day and a half to reach the hill where the spirits of our Zuni people go to rest after their deaths. When we reached our destination, a door led into the hill. This door has been seen only when the cults of the six kivas go there to offer the spirits blessings and in turn ask for the livelihood of the Zuni people. When these people came near the hill, there appears to be a door leading into four rooms that are designated as the way the Zuni people emerged onto the surface of the earth.

When we entered, we found the first room with floors of clean limestone. The doors were narrow and small. There in the first room we planted the prayersticks and came back out. The priests stood side by side along the places where they had planted their prayersticks. They told us, "Come, we will take you up on this hill to show you what lies on the other side."

We went up on the hill and looked over to see fields of corn, melon, and a great abundance of other crops. Then we came down the hill where the spirits of the Mudheads dwell. When we came farther down, we came to a spring where water ran free, down to the fields. After we saw the fields and came back to the spring, the two priests of the kivas, of which one was my brother, had to go into the spring. They undressed and took their sacred corn pouches and proceeded into the spring. When they neared the opening from which the spring came, they exclaimed that there had been someone who entered not long before them. The tracks proved to be those of a female.

The two men went on in murmuring prayers while they went on farther. As the priests went in, there came a flock of white geese coming down, joining with us. When the priests had finished their rituals in the spring and the rest of us completed what we were supposed to do, the priests came out and we started back home. But the flock of geese we saw has never again approached the spring. For the year we had gone to ask for blessings, we received rains, crops flourished, and there were no hardships. Only once had the flock of geese been seen and they were spoken of as a good omen.

Not long after, however, the priests became angry with each other, starting disputes that divided the Zuni people. There came many conflicts, and hardships grew to a point where the whole Zuni populace suffered.

Because of seeing the good omen, which was believed to be the source of prosperity, the Zunis every four years go to the Koh-thlou-wah-la-wah to give offering for the blessings of fertility of the land and peace among the Zuni people.

15   Famine in Zuni

During the time when the Zuni land was but a waste land, the people roamed about looking for food upon other lands. A man and his sister followed other small groups of Zunis migrating to other tribal lands. To Acoma they went. When they reached their destination, an Acoma man took them in and fed them. The two Zunis were content only for a short time. When the Zuni man spoke to his sister of marriage to one of the male members of the tribe, she agreed without any objections. So the Zuni man decided to talk to their keeper of his intention of marrying his sister off so they could get more food, for they had been fed only small, meager meals.

Came time for the Acoma man to go out for more kindling wood, the Zuni offered his assistance and was heartily invited to go along. They started out early in the morning, going about two miles out of the Acoma village, and began gathering wood. When they had finished, by noon, they sat down to eat their meal of corn cakes. The Zuni man spoke, "We have been kindly taken in by you and fed. I have come to think, if my sister were to marry one of your tribal members, we would be fed more than what we get now. We eat but seldom, and get just enough to keep us going until the next meal."

"I cannot say anything definite. We shall have to wait until we reach home and I have spoken to the elders and hear what they have to say about this."

So they came home and carefully laid out their bundles of wood, then they sat down to eat. The usual greetings were acknowledged and they had started to eat when the Acoma man spoke to the two elderly men sitting across from them. "If that is how he wants it, we shall think about this and shall give you our answer tomorrow." So they let that go until after the men discussed it.

That same night, after only a short agreement between the two, it was decided that one would marry her. The agreement was put to the Zuni girl and she accepted the decision with no qualms. So the Zuni girl came to be in charge of all meal preparation, seeing to it that she and her brother had all they wanted to eat.

While this was happening, Zuni was blessed with an abundance of rain that produced plenty of crops and food. As the exchange of visitors among the traders brought the news of Zuni and its improved condition, she approached her husband and asked, "I wish to return to Zuni and I have come to inquire if you would like to come with me or if you have any objections to coming with me."

"I have no objections, as it is right for the man to live with his in-laws, so whenever you are ready to go, we will start."

"Tomorrow we will go as soon as I prepare food to take along with us."

The preparation of food began and all the family left for Zuni. The goodbyes were said to the relatives of the Zuni girl's husband and they came on to Zuni. The Acoma man slowly became accustomed to the Zuni way of life and produced several offspring, and he became a respectable member of the Zuni tribe.

The famine led the Zunis into intertribal marriages that later on resulted in an increasing number of mixed-blood Zunis.

16 The Zuni and the Apache

Many years ago, a band of Apache came on a raid. Spending the night in "We-lok-lya," they aroused and woke early the next morning, as the Zuni warriors came out to their fields to water and weed their crops. The Zuni were not prepared when the Apache attacked them. The men ran to a little shed in the dugout at the side of the tall mountain. These men were saved as they shot at the Apache through small lookout holes in the walls of the little shed. Out farther, a young man was taken by surprise and killed. The Apache went on home while the Zuni men checked over their crops and came upon the young man, dead.

The men returned home for the day and one went to inform the dead boy's brother. When he was told, he took his gray prayerstick, for he was in the Clown Clan and the prayerstick was the object by which the clansmen received the power from the supernatural society and the spirits. He went out to the fields and indeed he saw his brother's body lying on its back. He dismounted and picked up a handful of sand from the tracks of the Apaches and put it in his dead brother's mouth. Then he turned the body over on its face and went after the Apache. As he rode on, he sang a song that was very sacred to the Clown Clan and that no one sang unless there were some new members initiated into the clan. Just as he was through with all his songs he sighted the Apache ahead.

The Apache noted the big cloud of dust following them; it seemed that an immense large group was coming after them. As the Apache fled, the Zuni lad with power from the supernatural caught up with them, raising such dust that nothing was visible. He went on into the party of Apache and ahead, waiting for them to come within range of his bow and arrows. He picked them off one by one as they came by him without seeing him. The Apache could not fight back at all, and when a party of Zuni came up from behind with arrows flying toward the Apache, they soon were all killed. The Zuni turned to take the trail home.

At that time, the Navajo and Apache settlements were not far to the north of the Zuni land, along the edges of the mountain cliffs and down into the village.

The Zuni, not yet satisfied with the lust to kill, came after the Navajo and Apache, killing great numbers. The roving tribes fled on farther north and each time they were attacked, they moved up north, and that is why there are no Navajo settlements to the south of our village today.

17 Mexicans Who Captured a Zuni Man

When the Spaniards first came to our lands, there was a man, Bynehahthle, a Bow Priest who was suspected of being a sorcerer. When the Spanish troops came, the Zuni told of Bynehahthle killing off most of his people. He did not actually kill anyone, but with his powers he enabled himself to cast spells on people, making them ill. When the troop's leader was informed of this he took the man into custody and wrote to his superiors in Mexico, telling of a man possessed of powers of the unnatural.

He was told to bring the man to Mexico to be punished for his crimes against his people. That they did; with a train of mules and a troop of soldiers, they proceeded down to Mexico. They spent many nights camped by or near water. Then they came to the coast near Old Mexico, where they spent another night before entering the city.

"Tomorrow we will reach our destination, but do not be afraid. Nothing will happen to you. I have grown fond of you, I shall help protect you. You will use the name Leo Hippo in the presence of our leader. If I am right, he would not harm one named as he is. The name he bears is a great one. You will be safe," the soldier assigned to Bynehahthle assured his captive.

Bynehahthle did not argue or question anything, so the night went by. First a large supper, then some soldiers recounted the more exerting events of their careers. When morning came, the troops marched into their city, going to their camp and to their assigned posts. As soon as the troops had settled down, the Zuni man was called with his guard. When they entered the Spaniard's chamber, the two knelt before him and soon they were questioned. "Is this the man who was brought from the low land?"

The guard answered, "Yes."

"What may his name be?"

"I do not know. Why not ask him?"

So the Spaniard asked and listened as the Zuni answered, "Leo Hippo." After a moment's silence, he repeated, "Leo Hippo." The Spaniard stood for a short while not believing the name spoken by the man.

"Alas! Man! You and I are blessed with the good name Leo Hippo. I cannot bring shame and degradation to so renowned a name. Tell me the truth, did you bring harm and fear to your people?"

"No, I have never done anything of the sort. All I did was get after them when they did wrong things, and I tried to talk to them."

"I believe you. I will not do anything to him. He bears the name of our father. He shall go free."

The Spaniard gave the command for the soldier to take off the chains on his wrists and when that was done, the Zuni was told to come back the following day.

Bynehahthle returned to the barracks with the troop and loafed about the rest of the day. At night, a big supper was served and singing came after that; then came dancing to rhythm of clapping hands. This lasted most of the night and into dawn. About mid-day, Bynehahthle went back to the Spaniard's palace, where he was ushered once more into the chambers. He was given a cane supposed to be blessed with supernatural powers with which he could bring prosperity, happiness, and peace to his people. Then he was sent back to the troops and soon they were on their way back to the Zuni land.

Bynehahthle was reminded by his guard to do only as their superior had instructed him: that if Bynehahthle were to do anything wrong against his people, the guard would be there to correct him, physically if necessary.

So they returned and no more was said about Bynehahthle.

18   The White Shoomehcoolie

One near point of death is sometimes healed by members of this clan. The person healed is then initiated into the clan. Women who are members of this clan may wear the masks.

When the villages of Hawikuh, Hehshokda, and Kechipbowa existed, once the people of Hawikuh desired to execute a ceremony to liven the spirits of the villagers. They had become bored with the quiet solitude of the village and began by first inquiring about the kind of ceremonial the people wanted. No one knew, so they were hesitant to speak their preferences. It was then decided that the Yellow Ant who dwelled in Kechipbowa would be called upon, for he had a brilliant mind and a great imagination. The Yellow Ant was summoned and he came forward at once. Upon his arrival he asked why he had been summoned. He was then told of the people's desire to perform some festivities to bring to life the spirit of the people: that there was nothing but solitude and a village so deathly still that there seemed to be nothing around; if there should be something happening, the people would be amused and so liven their spirits.

"So it shall be then. Our fathers who have gone beyond us we shall follow their patterns as a guide to the ceremonial we will do. When do you wish to carry this out?" the priests asked of their people.

"In four days, the time for scheduling will be set. Eight days will be set aside for the ceremony. When four of the days are up, we will make contact with the spirits of our fathers through our offerings of prayersticks. Four days following, the day for dancing will arrive and dancing shall commence all that day." The Bow Priests had declared the ceremony to be held, and for the next eight days prayersticks were prepared. Prayersticks for each direction of the earth were represented, also prayersticks for animals held sacred, then for the fathers of the earth, the supernatural beings who brought upon the earth all it possessed.

From the innermost place in the earth came the supernatural beings. They ascended upon the plaza in the village where the priests all awaited the appearance of these beings. There the offerings of prayersticks were given them, and so it was announced that the dances were to commence in four days.

The leader to head the dancing was chosen and the priests thought it only fitting that the Yellow Ant be the leader. Then his female relative, the Blue Girl, was to be his partner. The Black Ant was chosen to help the Yellow Ant and the Turquoise Girl was his partner. The supernatural beings departed and the villagers began preparations. Three days passed quickly and the day for dancing arrived.

The dancers came and in their designated order, the dancing commenced. The Yah Yah Dance was then performed.

From the world of the supernatural, one from the Shoomehcoolie Clan was sent to Hawikuh in the form of a White Shoomehcoolie. He was sent to perform the dance, bringing the spirits of the Great Fathers of the earth. Several days of dancing kept up and two of the spirits for whom the White Shoomehcoolie was to perform were left when he was dancing once more. When for the fourth time the Shoomehcoolie danced amidst the dancers, his thoughts were interrupted and he became anguished. As he stepped from the round of dancers, his leader sprinkled cornmeal ahead of him so he would go directly to his destination. Without warning, the Shoomehcoolie darted out and ran into the wooded hills. The dancers, alarmed, began to follow but could not catch up with him.

From the supernatural world, the last two Shoomehcoolie for whom the white one was dancing were sent to Hawikuh to follow the White Shoomehcoolie to Shebaboolima and bring him back, for the White Shoomehcoolie was not yet ready to go into the spirit world of the Great Fathers. He was being taken prematurely because the altar around which the dancing was taking place was not honored and held sacred as it should have been. The White Shoomehcoolie reached Shumingyah and there was stopped by the two Shoomehcoolie.

As this happened, the Yellow Ant, leading the dancing, came to life as a real Kachina, and the Blue Girl became a Mockingbird, while the Turquoise Girl was transformed into a Hummingbird.

The Mockingbird and the Hummingbird were told that from that day on, should anyone want to perform this dance, the leaders, with the help of the Mockingbird, should be cheerful and happy, bringing many people to participate and make merry. The Black Ant was told to roam extensively through valleys and that, should his people encounter anyone ill in health, they should with their weapons inject into the ill person the venom of life and good health.

It is from this happening that our people believe only in practicing these rituals by following the given patterns of the supernatural ones.

19 Zunis and the Outlaws

Early spring when the March winds were blowing furiously and the sandstorms blowing, covering everything, three white men came onto the Zuni land from the north. A Zuni man named Unaidi was herding sheep. As soon as he saw the three men approaching, he put his rifle in plain sight. As the men came nearer, they promptly noticed the gun, circled Unaidi a couple of times, and then headed out toward Shoondegyaah, where they camped.

As the three men left the man, they went along noting all the good horses grazing in the fields.

Then another man, Coona, was in the area. The white men came to him, friendly and nice, asking him to make them shoe soles out of rawhide. They wanted the soles of rawhide because it didn't leave imprints or tracks. But Coona didn't know this, nor did he care why the three men wanted the soles. He did as he was told.

While Coona was making the shoe soles, the three white men went out each day gathering the horses they had seen. About four days passed and the three men thought they had enough horses, so they broke camp and left, taking Coona with them. The horse thieves took every precaution to keep from being discovered of their thievery, but somehow, the Zunis had found out and organized a party to go after the thieves.

The thieves and their companion, Coona, came to a cliff dwelling. There, unaware that they were being followed, they stopped for only a short time. Suddenly the Zunis came and rounded up their horses, and two men brought them back to where they were. The Zuni men went after the white men, chasing them until the white men were driven through the village on out into the fields where the remaining Zuni men were working on their crops. There the Zunis increased their number and kept after the horse thieves.

A Bow Priest among the Zunis hesitated in commencing their fight against the thieves. So the horse thieves were chased out of view of the village, coming to small hills where they promptly took cover and fired at the Zunis. With the first shot, the Zunis killed the white men's companion, Coona.

The Zunis also took cover and started an exchange of fire. The horse thieves left their hiding place, going toward Nutria. A Zuni man was sent on a shorter route to Nutria with instructions to tell the men there to block the thieves. The man reached Nutria in a short time but did not bother to tell the men as he was instructed.

Daboo, another Zuni, sneaked around the horse thieves and went to Nutria after the men. He found the men working on their livestock corrals and told them what was happening. They immediately gathered their weapons and started out after the horse thieves.

The white men had entered a gulch and kept following it until they reached a small cabin at the base of the cliff. They entered it and hid themselves from the Zuni bullets.

As they exchanged fire, a Zuni was injured when a bullet hit his chin and it literally hung apart from his face. When that happened, the man asked for a knife to cut the part hanging but another man with him exclaimed that there would be nothing wrong with him after his wound healed.

Then as another man riding a horse raced across the line of fire, he was shot down and instantly killed.

The horses the white men rode were taken and the contents of the supply bags were given out equally.

As the fighting grew more furious, riders with instructions were sent to Fort Wingate, Nutria, and Zuni, asking for assistance. Without being asked, the Navajos came to aid the Zunis, but their help was refused because the Bow Priest would not allow the Navajos to kill the thieves. But the Navajos stayed, surrounding the area where the white men were.

The soldiers came from Fort Wingate as soon as they had been summoned, but they didn't want to assume the responsibility of the capture of the thieves. Instead, they challenged the Zunis to avenge the deaths of their fathers who had been killed by the white men. The Zunis refused, because the tribal ways of life forbade the willful taking of a life, no matter how justifiable. The soldiers were astonished to find the Zunis not willing to kill the thieves for killing their brothers and stealing horses.

A man named Jesus kept urging the killing of the murderers of their relatives, but the Zunis adamantly refused. The troops finally took the white men, only to release them when they reached Fort Wingate.

The three white men ran about free for almost a year. Then they came back to the reservation, this time to take Jesus and kill him, for it was Jesus's doing that they had been caught by the soldiers.

As they neared Jesus's sheep camp they saw a lone man herding sheep. They approached him, to find the man to be a Laguna. They asked many questions concerning Jesus's whereabouts and his activities. The sheepherder did not give the white men any information, claiming ignorance to anything Jesus did. The white men assured the sheepherder that they would find him, then they went on to where they had camped before.

Not long after the white men left, Jesus came back to his camp and his sheepherder told him of the three men looking for him. Immediately Jesus remembered the three white men whom they had fought with about a year ago and who had been taken by the soldiers. He asked his sheepherder for descriptions of each one of the men and his sheepherder told him, describing each: "A tall, slim man with a slightly crooked nose, a short man with a disfigured face, and a short man with a big black birthmark right beside his nose."

Positive that they were the same men, Jesus left his sheepherder and went back to his home. When he got there he told his wife about the men and persuaded his wife to ready herself so Jesus could take her to Pescado. It didn't take them long to reach Pescado, and there Jesus left his wife with some relatives and gathered the extra supply of ammunition, left his wagon, and started back for his sheep camp, riding bareback. When he came to his camp, he talked to his sheepherder.

"It is almost night, the sun is descending. Take the sheep and start home. I will be waiting for you. The food will be ready."

Jesus left his sheepherder and went back to his camp, and the Laguna man started rounding up the sheep and took them in the direction of the camp. Soon the men reached camp and sat down to eat. Jesus started talking.

"When you are through, you will first take your bedding to the west where there are sheets of limestone. There you will leave your bedding and come back to take the sheep to the new camp. The three men will probably come back tonight. You will be safe from any harm. I will stay here and wait for the white men."

After finishing supper, the Laguna man took his bedding and started walking to the west. He came back shortly to take the sheep back. At this time, Jesus chopped a large tree down, using the trunk to make coverings for the window openings. Then he chopped another tree and made a door to close the entrance to the house. Then, taking a long tree trunk, he placed it in the fireplace leading out to the chimney where he made himself a hiding place, also a good sighting area. He tried out the hiding place, finding it very satisfying. When he got back down from the chimney, he loaded his pistol and his rifle, putting an ample supply of bullets in his holster and then putting the remaining bullets in his pockets.

Just as the sun descended below the horizon, suddenly the

stillness was interrupted with the jingling of spurs and the small fixtures on the bridles and harnesses. Jesus heard, and went up to the top of the pole into the chimney. He looked out with only the top of his head showing. He watched the men dismount and approach the house with their pistols in their hands. Without bothering to check the inside of the house, the three men fired into the openings. They fired from every angle and for a long time the shooting was uninterrupted.

The sheepherder at his new camp not very far to the west heard the continuous firing and wondered how his friend could possibly survive the attack. As he sat fearfully listening to the noise, he thought of his Zuni friend, and the more he thought, tears rolled down his cheeks and he started crying until he was sobbing uncontrollably. The firing continued through the night. Then, finally, after they had been shooting the door for some time, the door was hanging loosely. They looked into the house and found no one, so they mounted their horses and started back.

When Jesus heard the slow beat of hoofs riding away he looked out and just as he got ready to shoot, the three spurred their horses and raced off into the darkness of the night.

Jesus did not bother coming out of the chimney but spent the rest of the night perched atop the pole in the chimney. Right at the break of dawn, the sheepherder came running into the house, his eyes full of horror at the sight of such massive destruction. As he stood in the center of the torn house, bewildered, down the chimney came his friend Jesus, covered with black soot from head to toe.

"Alas! My brother, you are still alive."

"Yes, just barely."

"Where are they now?" asked the sheepherder.

"They have gone. They headed toward the west when I saw them riding away," Jesus replied wearily.

"Yes, they were the same men we fought last spring. Well, let us eat now." The two men sat down to eat. They finished their morning meal in no time and Jesus went out and saddled his horse as his sheepherder stood looking at him.

"I am going after the three men," announced Jesus.

"Let them go. You are alone. They will be sure to take you and kill you," warned Jesus's sheepherder.

"No, I am going. Wait for me until noon, and if I don't come back by then, I will probably be dead," said Jesus.

Though the sheepherder protested, Jesus left after the white men. He followed their tracks into a bed of limestone where it was difficult to follow the tracks, but Jesus kept after the men and soon he was not very far behind them. As Jesus came farther west, he rounded a mountain and came to the Pierced Rock, and right beneath it he spotted the men. Two were sitting with their backs toward him and the other one was facing his direction. They were all eating. Jesus turned back a few yards and dismounted, tying the reins of his horse to a tree branch in case he had to depart in a hurry. Carefully he crept under trees, hiding behind small bushes, slowly but quietly making his way to a short distance from where the white men sat. He aimed his gun at one who had his back to him. He squeezed the trigger but hesitated, then decided to pray to the War Gods of the Zuni people, asking for courage and the spirits' help in his fight against the three men. When he had finished his prayer, he aimed at one of the two men and shot him and he fell dead. Then he quickly shot the other and also killed him. As the third one ran for cover, Jesus shot and killed him too. He took the corpses of the men and placed two of them on one horse and the other one on a different horse. Then he led the horses up to a cliff and threw the bodies over, as well as the saddles, packs, bridles, and harnesses.

While all of this went on, time passed and it was noon already. All this time his sheepherder kept looking to see if Jesus was coming back, but a short time after mid-day he started thinking about his friend again. He thought about Jesus's words, "If I am not back by noon, you are to assume that I am dead." Again the sheepherder started to cry.

Jesus had thrown over all the belongings of the white men, and thrown brush, branches, and dirt over the cliff to cover them. Then he took the three horses and led them east to not far from where the three men had been camped. He lined the horses under a tree and shot them. Again he gathered brush and branches, piling them on top of the dead horses. When he had enough wood and brush, he set fire to the pile, burning the horses. He stayed around a little longer, carefully covering any objects or disposing of anything that could be used as evidence against him.

In late afternoon he finally started home, satisfied with himself for what he had done and pushing his horse until the horse could no longer gain speed. It took quite a while before Jesus reached his sheep camp. The sheepherder, who had been out with the sheep, immediately ran back to the camp, glad to see his friend alive.

"Well, have you finished what you set out to do?" asked the sheepherder.

"Yes, I have taken care of the men. They are the same ones we fought, all right. But they will not be back to bother us again."

"There was another man looking for you this afternoon."

"What did you tell him?" asked Jesus.

"I didn't say anything but he kept saying that he wanted to see you."

Jesus thought for a moment and exclaimed, "There was another man, a big man, who tried rustling my cattle. I shot at him but I missed. Which way did he go?"

"He went to the east," replied the sheepherder.

"Well, I will wait a little while before I go after him. Bring your sheep back to the camp now. It is getting late," said Jesus. The sheepherder left to herd the sheep back into the corrals and Jesus went about fixing their supper. When the sheepherder completed his day's work, he arrived at the camp and the two men sat down to eat. Jesus rushed through his meal and soon saddled his horse, ready to go after the man who had asked his whereabouts.

Night had fallen and darkness prevailed over the forest. Jesus rode into the east, following a clear horse trail. About six miles west of El Morro, only a few feet from a water hole, sat the large man eating, the light of his campfire clearly outlining his silhouette. Jesus dismounted his horse and crept up closer behind the man and shot him from behind. He took the body and dumped it in a ravine, covering it with dirt and brush. He took the horse and brought it until he was not very far from his sheep camp. There he shot the horse and returned to the camp.

For a while, the Zunis were left peaceful and content, but again the horse thieves came, successfully taking only one horse.

The other Zuni men, although Jesus had taken care of the three men, were set on avenging the deaths of two fellow Zunis, Coona and another, each by his own method. So not long after the two white men who stole the horse had gone, a group of Zuni men gathered and went to look for the horse.

Not far from Nutria lived a man, Coweuca, who took his two young nephews along with him to look for their horse, instructing them, "I am going down after the men with our horse. Watch and see what happens. If the white men should get angry and perhaps kill me, do not do anything rash. Do not make any noise. Follow the trail you came on, back to your home. Then if need be, get help and come back after me tomorrow."

Coweuca left his nephews and went on down ahead. Without any words spoken, Coweuca came between the two white men, coaxing the horse back from the direction he had come. But the white men kept after the horse and then the three men started to fight. The white men grabbed Coweuca, pushing him to the ground, but he came back up, grabbing a leg of each of the two horse thieves and dragging them off their horses. He pinned them to the ground until each was under the weight of Coweuca. They struggled until they were free from the pressure holding them down. Then one of the white men took a knife and struck Coweuca in the hip and again in the shoulder. The blade broke as it lodged in the shoulder blade. The white men were frightened off when Coweuca took out his pistol and aimed it at them. He shot the two horses the white men were riding and then dragged himself over to the horse the two had stolen. With the gun pointed at the men, he took the reins of the horse and headed for his two nephews.

When the two young boys saw their uncle coming up, they came down to help him. Then they came west, stopping to rest near a mountain. The two boys had grown tired and the younger of the two started to cry from thirst. Not very far behind them came the white men, with their saddles upon their backs. Coweuca took his nephews on his back and started back to the small water hole behind them. As they came within sight of the water hole, he saw the two men lying a few yards from the pond. They waited until the fire went down to get some water. When they came back shortly, Coweuca went back after the two. He crept to them and searched their pockets and when he couldn't find anything, he left the two men and came back to his nephews.

They mounted their horses and came home through the darkness. They reached Nutria before dawn and lit the fireplace until it was very light in the house. A neighbor, unable to go to sleep, was standing looking out through a window and saw the house lit up. He awoke his wife and told her he thought he should go over to see if anything was wrong.

Coweuca had put his nephews to bed and was sitting by the fireplace when Weydo entered the house.

"Where have you been? You must have done something, for you to be coming at this time of the night."

"No, I didn't do anything. I did not kill the two white men who stole my horse because they didn't have anything on them so I let them go."

"You must have. You brought their guns with you," Weydo said, and he stood looking at the guns.

Weydo took a pair of wire cutters and took the broken blade out. As Coweuca let the shoulder get warm it started to hurt and the pain knocked him out. Weydo stayed at Coweuca's home until the wound healed.

Then they went out after the two men, but turned back for Nutria after they saw that the men had gone back up north out of the reservation.

Their lives were again back to normal until the next horse thieves or cattle rustlers would try their foolish deeds against the Zunis.

In the days of outlaws and lawlessness, the Indians were

stronger than any white man alive. Perhaps it was the way the Indians were, dependent on the strength their supernatural beliefs brought them, but one way or another, the Indians always got their revenge for any wrong done against them.

For time immemorial, the Zunis have respected the rules and laws of different tribes of men, but without consideration for the feelings of these people, many intruders have come only to be ingloriously defeated and sent away.

20 Zunis and the Outlaws

In the spring a group of outlaws headed by Red Pitkins held up a train near Fort Wingate. After they successfully hauled away the stolen money they came down to Towayalane and camped by the Corn Cob Ridge above some fields. Down in the fields was a corn crop growing successfully, and a man working his crops, where they accidentally came upon him. He was friendly to them and they took the man in as their companion and their keeper. He became attached to them and so was constantly aware of everything that might harm or endanger his friends. He looked after them faithfully, preparing their meals, mending their clothes, repairing their shoes and tools, while the outlaws roamed the country.

Then came the time for the Zunis to round the horses up and drive them to a place in the mountains. But when they sent a rider ahead to locate the herd of horses he found that a white man had rounded up the horses. The rider suspected the man of being an outlaw and waited until the man led him to a place where the outlaws were keeping camp. The Zuni man wasted no time informing his companions about his findings. He came to a group of Zuni men, shouting the news excitedly. They immediately formed a group to go after the outlaws. Without discussion or questions the Zunis rode madly, crossing the Black Rock Lake, going to Towayalane.

The outlaws herding the horses had noticed the man following them, so they notified their partners about the Zunis. Within a very short time the outlaws broke camp and headed east, the direction from which they had come. They raced their horses up through the Corn Cob Ridge and on further by the Pierced Rock and across Burnt Water. There had been a mild breeze when the outlaws started out, but as they progressed the wind became stronger and blew dust. Soon this wind became a dust storm, slowing the horses to a walk. Visibility was obstructed and the outlaws could not see where they were going. As they came to a deep, dry gulch near Nutria, they entered and followed on down to the south. The Zunis gained much distance and were right behind them. A Bow Priest heading the men ordered the outlaws killed as soon as they could be caught. The Bow Priest had no idea of how to shoot a musket or any other kind of weapon. But the Bow Priest would have to shoot the first shot before any fighting commenced.

As the outlaws came to a lumber mill, they came out of the gulch and on up into the hills of Nutria, and the Zunis came upon them.

During those times, clusters of houses around Nutria were situated in the niches of the mountains, leaving only one exit from the house. There the outlaws hid from the weapons of the Zunis, firing at the Zunis until they retreated, but this was not until the Zunis had killed one of the outlaws. When the Zunis retreated the outlaws made a run for the gulch again. They sought a place where they could find refuge, but they were pursued nevertheless. They entered a small area where a massive growth of willows forced the band to separate. It was here they were surrounded. The Zunis lassoed Red Pitkins's horse and he was pulled to the crowd of Zuni men. There he was harshly reprimanded before the Zunis were to carry out their intentions of killing him. Red Pitkins broke away, and again they were chased until they rounded a small hill. Here they ducked and started a bombardment of bullets on the Zunis. The Zunis were left out in the open and as each scrambled to bushes or to boulders for safety, a deaf man among the Zunis was shot. This is what set the Zunis off into a rage, making them fight a battle with the odds against them. So courageously did they fight that the efforts were proven to be of acute victory.

    The outlaws made their way out into the gulch and again one by one they went along the walls, coming to a small cliff. At the base of the mountains stood a small log cabin. There the outlaws ducked in for shelter, while the Zunis once again tried to attack. One of the outlaws stayed out, standing behind the door, shooting at the Zunis. A short distance from the house a Zuni man named Whosondonia, herding his sheep, heard the commotion of men shouting and the fire of their muskets.
He left his flock of sheep and came to see what was happening. As he came up from a small hill he saw the outlaws, especially the one behind the door. Aiming his musket, he was ready to shoot. Just as the outlaw squeezed the trigger on his musket, Whosondonia fired, missing the outlaw by a hair but killing the horse. As the horse fell to the ground one of the Zunis shot

and killed the outlaw. There was a pause in the exchange of fire, but only for a minute, before the outlaws continued the barrage of bullets on the Zunis. The Zunis started to spread out around the cabin, hiding behind boulders and bushes.

While all the fighting was going on, one of the Zunis had ridden to Fort Wingate to bring the soldiers to Nutria to subdue the outlaws. On his way he met a troop of soldiers approximately ten miles north of Nutria, checking the wells and the grazing lands. The Zunis told the soldiers about the outlaws and the troops immediately headed for Nutria.

They rode furiously through the forest, following a small trail, never slowing their pace, and within three hours the troops came to find the outlaws securely surrounded and guarded by the Zunis. The outlaws shot at the troops and the Zunis, but shortly exhausted their ammunition supply, which caused them to give themselves up without further struggle. The troops apprehended the outlaws and immediately took them to Fort Wingate, where they waited two weeks before the outlaws were tried for the holdup on the train.

Two Zunis had been taken as witnesses against the outlaws on the charges of horse stealing and murder. While the trial was going through the preparation process some Zunis had gone up to Fort Wingate to see what was happening. Reaching the fort, they found the outlaws and the Zuni men in a log cabin awaiting their turn to be interrogated. When the interrogation was over, a judge presiding over the case called in each witness to identify the outlaws as the ones stealing the horses and firing at the Zunis. The Zunis immediately pointed Red Pitkins out as the aggressor and the thief, and then followed through recognizing the rest of the band of outlaws. When that was done, the charges brought against them were not denied. They were convicted and sentenced, then jailed in Luna, New Mexico. The duration of the sentence was never made clear, so it is not known what happened to the outlaws.

III FABLES

21 The Coyote and the Badger

Once upon a time there lived a coyote with his grandmother, because he had left his wife and his in-laws. Not far from where the coyote lived, at the dwellings of the badgers lived one with its wife.

One nice day, the coyote decided to go hunting. At that same moment, the badger also decided to go hunting. They went out, going over their hunting grounds. They hunted in areas close to their homes for a short time, then they went farther out and found one another. They immediately became friends.

"Oh, my friend," called out the coyote.

"What are you doing?" asked the badger.

"I am hunting."

"I am also hunting. Why not go around hunting together? I am fast. I will catch the game for you and you will be my Syyaqueh."

"But what will I use as Syyaqueh?"

"No, no! It is not like that. When I get the rabbits, you will carry them for me. That is what a Syyaqueh is. A rabbit carrier."

"Well! Sure, I will do that."

The two went on their way, the badger getting the rabbits out from their holes and the poor coyote trying unsuccessfully to catch any sort of small game. Instead of catching any, he chased them away. The badger easily caught quite a few rabbits and the bundle on the coyote's back became bigger and heavier.

As they came down, Etsuwahkkya, the badger, went to a small water hole. The coyote was then chasing a rabbit farther away from the badger. The badger had become tired of the coyote's blundering, so he took the bundle of rabbits and started out, saying to himself, "Oh! He can do what he likes, I am going home." The badger went on, leaving the coyote far behind.

When the coyote got through chasing the rabbit, he came to the place where he had left the badger and found no one around. For a moment he panicked, but quickly collecting himself found the tracks of the badger heading home. The coyote followed the tracks as fast as he could and came to another water hole, where he caught up with the badger. He could not hold his anger back, so he shouted, "Hey! Why did you come ahead without me? You have one of my rabbits. Maybe you are trying to run away with it!"

"No! I am not doing anything of the sort."

The coyote cooled off and exclaimed, "Aren't you hungry? Let us eat here."

"I have already eaten. I threw half a tortilla into the water. Why don't you go after it?"

The moon had come out and was shining its light brightly on the water. The piece of bread was clearly floating on the surface and the coyote saw it.

"Yes! I see it!" The coyote dove into the water with a big splash and swam after the bread. Each time the coyote thought he was close enough to get the bread, he would surface and find the bread a short distance away. He tried several times but he finally gave up and came back to the bank. He looked about but did not see the badger anywhere.

When the coyote had jumped into the lake, the badger once more had put his bundle of rabbits upon his back and run on ahead. The coyote was furious. He ran after the badger muttering to himself. As the badger neared his home, the coyote caught up with him.

The moon had been faintly covered from view by the rolling clouds, and a small breeze was pushing the clouds slowly across the face of the moon as the badger looked up at the sky. He was leaning against the side of a mountain as the coyote came running up to him. Again the coyote shouted in anger, "You ran without me again! I chased all these rabbits so you could get them without having to chase them. I am tired but I will fight you."

"No! Don't do that. I am tired also. Look over here. The cliff is about to fall over and I am trying to hold it up."

The coyote looked up and saw the clouds moving and the mountain looked as if it were ready to fall over.

"Yes, I will help you," the coyote shouted, and quickly stood himself against the side of the mountain and pushed with all his strength.

"You keep pushing and let me rest a little while." The badger walked around the side of the cliff and ran, leaving the coyote pushing himself against the cliff. The badger ran on home to his wife. The wife was delighted to see the big bundle of rabbits and exclaimed, "Oh, my! You killed many rabbits today, didn't you?"

"Yes, I had a good day."

Back at the cliff the coyote was getting tired, and hollered out for the badger to come relieve him.

"Hey, come take over."

No one answered, and the coyote yelled out once more, and silence followed again. He yelled yet again and when no one came he turned around and saw no one.

"He must have run home. That no-good badger." The

coyote ran, winded by his anger, but he did not stop for anything. He ran until he came to the badger's home and yelled into the burrow, "You badger, give me my rabbits."

"You are mad! I killed them so they are mine."

"You liar! I killed some too! Give them to me!"

"But they are mine!"

"No, not all of them. Now give me some. If you don't I will eat you up."

"I killed them so they are mine. You only chased them. I had to dig them out of their holes. I did all the work."

Back and forth the two argued until the badger's wife said, "Oh, go and throw out a couple for him!"

The badger reluctantly threw two small rabbits out of their opening.

The coyote, ravenously hungry from all his running, ate the rabbits in only a few moments. When he finished, he was in much better spirits. He called into the hole and spoke, "I am going home now."

The coyote started home. When he reached the hills a short distance from their home, he rolled in the sand, curled himself up in a tight ball, and went into a deep sleep.

Along came a pack of mice and they started to chew on him. The coyote was in such a deep sleep that he did not feel the mice chewing on his fur. When he finally woke up, he found himself hairless, and his skin shone like that of a plucked chicken. He guessed who had done that, so he went right to the mice. He called into the holes asking, "You mice down below, are you the ones that took all my hair off?"

"No, it must have been the field mice. Why don't you go see them?"

The coyote bounded off to see the field mice, but they denied having anything to do with the coyote. They suggested he go to the groundhogs. So he went to them and found they had not done anything. There he was told to go see the pack rats. They too denied the accusation. Angered, the coyote threatened them.

"Do you want me to close your hole?"
"With what would you do that?"
"With twigs of cedar. Then you won't be able to get out."
"Hah! That is our food. Our parched meal."
"But I am still going to close your entrance."
"With what?"
"With the corn husks."
"Hah! That is what we make our meal chips of."
"But I shall close your hole."
"With what?"
"Dry corncobs."
"Hah! Did you not know we make bread patties from those?"
"Well, I will still block your entrance."
"With what?"
"With sagebrush."
"Ha, ha! That is our food also."

The coyote gave up and went away. He roamed about until he came to a water hole. He swam about for a short time, then came out of the water and went to a wild bean patch. There he found balls of fluffy white fur on top of the plants. He shook the furry flakes from the balls. The coyote rolled to the ground and the furlike flakes stuck to his body. He thought to himself, "Yes, my fur is almost like before. It does not show that I have been bald." Satisfied with his new coat of hair, he went home.

Because of what the coyote did, his followers now have fur a color between white and tan. At one time their coats were all evenly tan.

22 The Whip

In the days of long ago there lived the two little War Gods Ahauda, with their grandmother, at Shopthlouwahah. The two little War Gods would go to the wide culvert and play there. Each day the children from Halona would come also, but for them, the whip would come out and whip them, so they would not stay.

The grandmother warned her grandsons not to go to the wide culvert, for there was a whip that whipped the children of Halona when they came to play there. She was afraid her grandsons, too, would be whipped if they came upon the whip.

The grandsons assured their grandmother they would not go, but as soon as she went back to the house, the little War Gods scampered over to the wide culvert. They came upon their playground and took notice of a large oven that stood on top of a mound, and there inside it was the whip, lying in a large coil with its head in the center.

"Let us go see the oven."

"Grandmother said that is the place where the whip lives."

"Yes, I know, so let us go see it," said the younger brother to the other.

The other War God hesitated. "Oh no! The whip might whip us."

"No, it won't," assured his brother, "we will hide from it and it won't be able to find us."

"Oh, all right," the War God said.

So the two crept up to the oven silently and carefully peeked in through a small opening. There they saw the whip in a tight curl, sleeping.

"Hey, he does live here," the War Gods said in amazement.

"Let me wake it up," the other little War God whispered excitedly. "We can hide from it behind the little embankment here."

"All right, then."

So the little War Gods yelled at the whip, "Hey, whip, come out and whip us."

From inside the oven the whip answered, "Who is that, calling to be whipped?"

The whip uncoiled itself and looked out, but could see no one, so returned and lay in its oven. Twice the whip was called out but returned when it could see no one.

The other War God said, "Now I will call in to the whip and this time we will run toward the south. It surely cannot be long enough to reach us." The other agreed. So they tramped up to the oven and called in once more, "Hey, whip! Come out and whip us."

The two ran fast and far, but the whip came up from behind them and lashed itself against the one lagging a little distance behind the other. As it came down upon his back, the War God cried out, "Oooowwwch! It hurts badly to be whipped."

The two War Gods ran faster and came around a large boulder where they hid from the whip. The whip ran toward the east but lost sight of the War Gods.

"It is all out now. Let us fight it back now."

The whip then came after them. As one of the War Gods ran, he took out a blade of turquoise, which he threw at the whip, and it immediately slashed the whip several times, and short strips of the whip came off. The whip then returned to the oven. There its life ended.

The War Gods, satisfied with their destruction of the whip, said to it, "There now, this is what we wanted to do to you. Because of you, the little ones of Halona were forever crying.

Now, the will of everyone has been done. There will be children to play without fear of the whip."

They came back to their grandmother and asked her to look at their backs. She saw there were deep gashes left by the whip.

"Hey, why are you bruised like this?"

"We were whipped by the whip."

"Goodness! Did I not tell you to keep away from its oven?"

"We went, but we fixed it good. We have killed it. It came after us and whipped us. But when we ran away and came to the Greasy Hill we took out our turquoise weapon and slashed it to pieces and now it is dead."

"Well, that is good. You did well by bringing it to an end. Now the children of Halona will no longer cry from the whipping of the whip. But my grandsons, you are indeed senseless. Therefore, we cannot all stay here because you are the way you are. But I have grown old here, so I shall remain where I am now. The future generations of our people can come and seek the blessings of bounty and fertility by giving offerings to me of sacred cornmeal."

To the younger of the War Gods she said, "And you, little brother, will go up to Towayalane, where you will stay. When the young people offer cornmeal you will receive it. When the time comes, both of you will be blessed. From your locations, you will look after your people and the land also." So then the three separated, to stay where they could best serve their people.

From then on, when times of want and need came upon the people, they went to the place of the War Gods and their grandmother with offerings of cornmeal and prayers that they be delivered from their want.

23   The Ghost

A fable used to frighten children into obedience.

 Long ago, when every one of the people lived here in one village, our children, who defied the authority of their elders, brought upon themselves the beings derived from the powers of the priests.

 The children, young boys and girls, heeded nothing and continued their follies around the kiva in the center of the village. The priests warned them time and time again, but to no avail. Then when the priests had been tried and their tolerance exhausted, they gathered and discussed the situation.

 The House Master, who belonged to a Kachina Clan, put forth his thoughts and announced what he was going to do. None of the other priests objected, so the House Master told them, "Starting tomorrow night, there will come a ghost and for the next three nights, it will continue to come." To one of the Bow Priests he instructed, "You will go out and inform your people. You will tell them of the ghost and that it is coming to make the people realize the value of their ancestors' ways. You will tell them that unless they start showing respect for their elders and the rituals of religious ceremonies, they, the people, will bring upon themselves destruction."

 The priests discussed other things and shortly they left for their homes. The House Master entered another room where he began to prepare himself, then went on to eat the cornmeal. Finished, he went out of the village to the burial site of an uncle who had died at the hands of an enemy. There he dug a small hole and laid in it the food he had brought along. As he did this he prayed to his uncle, telling him of the plans.

A month later, from behind the place where the food had been placed, the uncle who had died came alive again. The ghost came directly to the little hole and through moans and weeping it ate all the food. Then when the ghost had finished, it spoke to the House Master. "What brought you here? Or have you something important to tell me?"

"Yes," answered the nephew, "I have something to say, I wish to please speak my part."

So the House Master of the priests told of the young children who kept up the uproar of noise, and said, "The children are making it very difficult for us to make a decision." He then talked about how everyone who had gone out to admonish them had been mocked, or at times even attacked with violent assaults; how, after much thought and consideration, the House Master thought he had come up with an idea that could solve their problems.

The ghost agreed to the plan, so they decided that four days later it would come upon the people in the village and for four nights would do as instructed.

The House Master returned to the kiva and informed the Bow Priests to call out to the villagers and inform them that the ghost would appear on the fourth night and that following that day, it would continue to come for the next three, in an effort to bring peace and quiet to the village. They were advised to feed upon the luxuries they had stored away for feasts and celebrations, because they might not have a chance to use what they had; they might not survive what was to be brought upon them.

The women immediately brought out from their well-hidden closet-type chests large quantities of dried fruits, peaches, apricots, baked corn, and whatever else they had. They made stacks of tortillas with a meal of precious corn. Everything was cooked and prepared; for the next four days they ate very well.

When the day came, once more the Bow Priests went out and called to the people to use caution, for this ghost would surely come unlike anything they had ever seen or imagined. After the last meal, the village quieted, except for the young boys. Shortly after, the House Master had gone into the other room where he ate some cornmeal and started out toward his uncle's grave site. There the ghost was prepared to come. After prayers, the ghost started for the village, while the House Master waited. Just outside the village, the ghost wailed hauntingly and chanted a song. Back at the grave site, the House Master heard an eerie shrill all over the village, and chills ran up and down his back. He declared himself that what was taking place was of his doing and that it was right, and so affirmed, he would not bring it to an end.

The ghost chanted the song four times as it progressed closer to the village, and the sound became louder as it came to the corrals, a short distance up from the river. The village was then in a tight cluster. The dark alleys that lay within the village went east and south from the main plaza. At that moment, a man had come out of his house and sat by the door, as the sun was bidding farewell to the world for the day. Then all at once the chant sounded. He sat there listening intently and heard the sound again.

The moon was shining brightly overhead and the shadows began reflecting monstrous images. Another man came out, and the man sitting down declared he had heard weird noises. Directly, as if on cue, the sound came again. They stood in shock, numb with fright at the sound of the chant. Then the ghost appeared, and with it came a cloud of mist. The men remained motionless and silent, so the ghost went farther.

The ghost went back to the House Master's house, where it

came to a stop for the night. The House Master came home, and in the dark and still of the night, he ate more cornmeal and then retired for the night.

Meanwhile, another man came along and found the two men in a state of shock. He started to try and awaken them, but it was useless. Finally the men regained consciousness and they told of what they had seen. From another direction, the sound of laughter from the group of boys near the plaza sounded loud and clear. The men, angered by this sudden outburst, approached them quickly and advised them to quiet down. They were only mocked by the boys and thrown from the booing group.

The three men decided to wait for the ghost until the next night and see if they could capture it. They left the crowd and went home. The next night, the men and a few boys from the crowd went out to where the ghost had appeared the previous night. They all held hands securely to prevent the departure of the ghost, but as it appeared, once more it sang the chant, and they all froze in their tracks, unable to either move or utter a sound.

The ghost reappeared and went through the line of defense, and along with it went the mysterious cloud. After a period of time, the men regained consciousness but were unable to comprehend what had happened. So twice the ghost had come and gone. Even though frightened, the men were sure they could apprehend the ghost the following night.

The next night the men separated into two groups, stationing from one point of entry to the other. They assured each other that they themselves would not be scared after having already seen the ghost. So the men once more joined hands and waited as the ghost wailed the haunting song. As it did this it came closer. The men who had seen the ghost stood sure of themselves, while the others braced themselves against this horrible sight. The men stood ready and once more the torn, bloodied remnants of a man came upon them and went through the line of defense. The group at the departing point tried to keep the ghost from leaving, but it was of no use, for it could not be felt as it passed through their guarding line.

Defeated and anxious about their future, the men gathered and affirmed they would try their best to apprehend the ghost, for they believed that if they did not capture the ghost their people and the village would be doomed.

On the fourth day the women and everyone else, scared to the point of hysteria, rushed about trying to keep themselves busy. Through the day, crying was heard in the village and some of the people sobbed at the thought of destruction, which they were sure would fall upon them within a short while.

As the sun began to set, the men formed a large gathering. They split up into groups to be at different points of the village, surrounding the area upon which the ghost had trod the night before. They instructed one another and soon were prepared. A short time later the ghost was heard, and once more the wailing of the chant began. As the chant faded away, the men clasped their hands and stood facing the entrance into the plaza.

The ghost came as though carried by a strong wind. The men standing there were pushed out of the way. Some clung to the rags covering the bloodied figure. As more men clung upon its rags, it was no longer able to lift itself, so the ghost came to the ground in the plaza. The men begged to be made known the reason for the ghost's appearance, and while the men threw questions upon the ghost, they heard the sounds of the young boys coming from inside the kiva. The men decided to bring the ghost upon the young boys, so it was led upon the roof of the kiva. Then the ghost was released, and it descended upon the boys, wailing as it approached them. The boys fainted from the shocking sight. As the ghost circled the kiva several times, the men entered and brought it to rest. Then the men brought back the young men to consciousness, whereupon the boys began to cry and wail from fright.

The men pondered what they were to do with the ghost. Finally it was decided that it should be taken to the priest, where the purpose of its appearance would be clarified to them. The ghost was set before the priest and was unclothed where they came upon it, dressed in the costumes of the four Kachinas. When the last mask was taken off, the face of the dead uncle was brought to light and it spoke.

"As each night our priests gathered to speak of important religious matters, they were interrupted by the noises and outbursts of the young boys. The people began to lose their sense of values and standards, which had dominated our lives, brought on to us by our ancestors. Tonight, of all the people here, you would have been doomed, but because of the blessings you received from our fathers, you have been delivered from an ill fate. But let no more of this improper conduct be continued. You will live in calm and order. But if you should persist toward the unwanted and undesired, there would be no alternative but for another of my kin to come upon you and there shall be no hope for you then."

The ghost was given prayersticks in offering and clothed with the Kachina mask, then it was led out of the kiva and proceeded back to the grave site where the House Master waited. The ghost, having done what was requested of it, clasped hands with the young man, and together they entered the grave, whereupon their spirits came to rest at Koh-thlou-wah-la-wah.

So, this was told to us by our grandfathers when we were

growing up, and the fear of the ghost kept our village in order and also calm. But calm is not known to us any longer, for our young roam about at night and into the early morning hours, producing the most inconceivable sounds brought upon us by the advancement of times.

24   Turkey Maiden

Long ago there lived a maiden in a village called Matsakya, where she had a flock of turkeys to tend. One day while tending her flock she heard of a Yah Yah Dance which was to be held at the village plaza. The next day she was fixing a meal for her sisters when one of them asked her if she wanted to go and see the dance. She replied, "I don't know, I have nothing nice to wear." So the other two sisters left for the dance. Shortly after, she went down to get her flock out to feed. When she got there, to her surprise, one of the turkeys spoke to her and asked if she was going to the dance. She told the turkey that she didn't have nice things to wear. "Have no fear, my child," said the turkey, "go wash up, come back, and we will get you ready in time to go see the dance." So she ran to the house with joy. Soon she was back at the pen. With three magical songs of the flock, the turkeys turned her into a beautiful maiden. They told her to hurry back after the fourth dance and let them out to be fed.

When she got to the dance, one of her sisters saw her and asked the other sister, "Could this be our sister?" The other sister replied, "How could it be, she didn't have a thing to wear." "But it is her that's standing there," said the other sister, "I'm going to see for sure." So she went to the place where she was standing. Sure enough, it was her sister. They greeted each other and the other sister asked her if she had locked the pen where the turkeys were. She replied, "Yes, I did, and I was told to be back after the fourth dance." While they were still talking, the dance had already started. So they danced the first dance. After it was over they went to the place where the other sisters were. They danced the second dance, then the third and the fourth. She got so interested that she forgot all about the warning from the flock. While dancing the fifth dance she remembered, and told her sisters that she had to leave.

Meanwhile, the flock flew out of the pen and fed around the pen, then wandered off to the hills. The maiden returned to the pen only to find it empty. She started to look and a few hours later she found the turkeys at the top of the hill. They told her that she had disobeyed them and for that reason they were flying away. They flew to the other hilltop, and again the maiden went after them. When she reached them, they flew off and landed on the field. By this time the maiden was very tired, but still she went after them. They flew away and landed to drink in a spring flowing out of the rocks. The maiden was so tired that she gave up and went home. The turkeys were full of joy because they were free and could go anywhere they wished. To this day you see the tracks of the flock where it drank at the spring.*

---

*History tells us that long ago the world was young and soft. But as the years went on, it hardened, so that's why we have lots of fossils in this world of ours.

IV FABLES OF MORAL INSTRUCTION

25   The Priest's Son and the Eagle

There lived a little boy with his sister and his parents. They owned many fields where they raised crops. The boy's father was a priest for the people in the village. One morning when the boy left his home to go to his fields he walked around his fields and found an eagle's nest. He saw a little eagle in the field and caught it and said to himself that he was going to take the eagle home with him.

When he arrived home he made a house for the eagle and kept it for a pet. His mother asked, "Why are you coming back so early?"

The boy told his mother, "I brought an eagle home and I'm going to keep it." The next day, early in the morning, the boy went out to hunt for food for his eagle. He killed a rabbit and went home to feed his eagle. When he took it to the eagle, it was very pleased with the rabbit and ate it all up.

After that the boy went out to get water for his eagle. By the time he was all finished hunting it was almost sundown. So he rested for the night. The little boy kept up with his hunting every day for his eagle. In the mornings he went hunting for rabbits and in the evenings he got water for his eagle.

While the boy went hunting every day, his father went to work in his fields. The boy had helped his father every day to work in their fields until he found the eagle; then he quit helping his father and started hunting for the eagle. Several days later the little boy's father said to him, "I don't like what you are doing. I'd rather have you help me work in the fields instead of going hunting for rabbits."

The eagle overheard the father and was disappointed. The boy's father wasn't happy when the boy came home with another rabbit. He wanted to feed it to his eagle, but the eagle didn't eat it because it wasn't happy. The boy wondered why the eagle didn't want the rabbit and what had happened to it.

He went to his house to eat supper and after supper he came out to see his eagle again. The rabbit was still where he had left it, and the water was also there. The eagle hadn't eaten the rabbit at all and hadn't drunk the water. So the boy asked his eagle, "Why haven't you eaten or drunk?"

Much to his surprise the eagle talked to the boy and told him why it wasn't happy, that it had overheard the boy's father say that he didn't like for him to go hunting for the eagle. The eagle said, "It is because of you. You haven't been helping your father with the crops."

The eagle got angry and asked the boy to let it out of its cage so it could go live someplace else. But the little boy said, "I will go with you."

At first the eagle told him he couldn't go, but the boy insisted that he wanted to go with the eagle. Finally the eagle said, "Okay, you can come with me, but you have to bring some bells with you." So the boy went into his house and got two bells. They were little bells and he put one on each of its legs with a string.

A few minutes later the boy and the eagle flew away together, with the boy sitting on the back of the eagle. At that time the boy's father, mother, and sister were working in their fields. As the two were flying, they flew by his father's fields and saw his parents and sister. So the eagle told the boy to let his parents know that he was going away. So the boy started to sing a song. As he was singing his little sister heard, so she stopped to listen. Once again her brother started to sing. His sister found out that it was her brother singing because as the boy sang, he called out his Indian name. That's why his sister knew that it was her brother singing. Then she told her parents and they all listened. Sure enough, it was their boy singing and telling them that he was going away from home with his eagle.

After the father heard that his boy was going away he wasn't happy, and he was sorry for what he had said about the eagle. But there was nothing he could do. It was too late to stop him. The eagle kept flying with the boy on its back until they reached the eagle's home. When they got there all of the other eagles were sitting inside of their homes. So the eagle flew in with the boy and greeted the rest of the family.

The eagle family was pleased to see their other eagle coming home, as it had been gone for several days. The eagles noticed that it was bringing a boy home. The eagles weren't like the eagles of today. The eagles, a long time ago, used to turn into people and talk. By their magical ways they changed from eagles to human beings. When they went outside to hunt for food they turned into eagles but when they stayed inside their houses they were like people. That's why after the boy decided to go with the eagle and live with it and the rest of the eagle family, they made him marry their sister, so he could stay with the eagles.

During the day the boy and his wife stayed home while her brothers went out to hunt for food. Several days later the boy's wife turned herself into an eagle and the boy sat on her back, then they flew out together. As they were hunting they killed a deer. Because the boy's wife and her brothers were eagles they ate their meat raw, but the boy cooked his meat.

Then one day the couple went out together again. Each time when it was time for them to eat they built a fire together and the boy cooked his meat. His wife always waited for her brothers to come so they could all eat together, but they didn't cook theirs; they ate theirs raw.

As the days went by the wife decided to take him to another place and see their friend. They call their friends their grandfathers and grandmothers. They went to the home of the cranes living on the other side of the mountains. They ate their meals cooked. So when the boy arrived there they fed him deer meat, and it was cooked. The boy stayed with the cranes until it was sundown, then he went back to his wife's place. His wife had gone hunting and later she brought home another deer.

As he went out for a walk each day he met two female hawks. He stayed with them, then he married one of them. There were some witches living on the other side of the mountain. One day when the boy went out for a walk he happened to stop where the witches lived. Later the witches found out that someone had been to their home. They followed the boy until they found him at the home of the eagles. The witches found him and tried to take him. The eagles fed him a spoiled meat, just so the witches wouldn't take him. The boy ate the meat even though it was spoiled, because if the boy didn't eat the meat, the witches would have taken him and killed him so he would become one of them, too.

Finally, the eagle family thought maybe it would be best if he went back to his parents. In the meantime, the boy's father, mother, and little sister were lonesome for him. His sister waited for him every day, hoping he would come home. She used to sit on top of her house by the ladder.

One evening her brother finally came home and the sister saw him coming. She rushed in to tell her parents, but at first they didn't believe her, so she went out again and watched her brother until he came near the house. The parents were so happy to see their boy home again.

Moral: Foolish bravery.

26   Little Arrowheads

Long before our grandfather's time, to the east there lived some little arrowheads. They danced every day to their father's song.

Not far from them a horned toad was hunting and eating ants and such. He was out on his daily hunt when he heard the singing of the arrowheads. He was curious about this, for he thought there was no one around these parts except the usual animals he saw. He stopped eating and went down a small trail toward the home of the arrowheads. He came upon the group shortly and observed the little arrowheads dancing and their father singing. The horned toad approached the arrowheads and exclaimed, "Alas! So you live here in joy and activity. I have never seen you around before."

"Yes, we live here and every day we dance, keeping ourselves busy and happy. You have surprised us because none from the village has ever seen us, and you are the first one to ever see us here," the father replied.

"I was out hunting and I suddenly heard your singing, so I came to see what it was I heard."

"Well, we are here every day."

"This is the first time I have come out in this direction and so I came upon you. You must dance some more for me because I really like your pretty songs." The horned toad looked on enviously and longingly. The arrowhead father turned to his children and said, "You will dance and make merry now. You will also dance in jest, so it will be a lot of fun." The father began to sing and the children danced to the merry tune. The horned toad looked as if he wanted to join in on the fun and dancing.

Once more the horned toad exclaimed about their joy and happiness, "You are really enjoying yourselves and I envy you the way you live. Now I must go home and bring my children over so they too can dance."

The horned toad departed and within a short time returned to his children and asked, "These children that are dancing, they might be your relatives. Would you like to dance with them?"

"We do not know, for we do not know how they dance. We shall see how they dance and then perhaps if we like it, we will join them."

The arrowhead father began to sing and the children danced and the others looked on. The little horned toads began to feel the joy and the happiness the little arrowheads spread over them with their dancing. Soon the little horned toads were asking if they could join the little arrowheads in their dancing. The tune stopped and the horned toads came into the round circle and were ready to start dancing. The arrowhead father started once more to sing the little tune he had been singing.

The dancing went on as the little horned toads danced

with all the enthusiasm and spirit they could put into the dancing. Then finally when they were too tired to move, the dancing was over and the little children exclaimed that they had never experienced such a time in their lives, that they were envious of how the little arrowheads lived.

With that, the horned toad decided it was time for them to go home. But before they left they invited themselves to another day of dancing, to come the next day.

For the next four days, the little horned toads and the little arrowheads danced and danced. When on the fourth day the dancing had ended, the father horned toad went out to hunt and found another anthill. As he proceeded to tear apart the anthill, the ants decided it was time they taught the toad a lesson. They decided to do away with the toad. Soon his body became swollen and shortly he was dead.

The arrowheads and little horned toads, struck with the death of their father, stopped dancing. Thereafter, no one in the forests danced, as they were afraid of the memory of what had happened.

You should not be a copycat. It never works out.

27 The Grasshopper and the Coyote

A long time ago at Hawikuh, on the west side, was a cornfield that the grasshopper grew. A coyote lived at the south side and she was an old coyote. One day she went out to hunt and she saw the cornfield and the grasshopper who sat and watched it. There were lots of corn, melons, and all kinds of vegetables.

As the old lady coyote came close to the grasshopper she heard the grasshopper singing.

"Oh, that is such a beautiful song. I would like to learn it and sing it for my grandchildren when they are ready for bed. I think I will go ask him to teach me the song," she said to herself, and then went down to the cornfield. When she came upon the cornfield she saw the grasshopper sitting in the shade.

"Whose vegetables and fruits are these?" she asked.

"They are mine," the grasshopper answered.

"What were you singing about?" she asked.

"I was praying for the vegetables to grow fast," he told her.

"I heard you singing, that is why I came," she said. "You sing for me and I will learn it and I would like to sing it for my children," the coyote told him.

The grasshopper said, "You sit down here and listen so you will learn." Then the grasshopper sang. After he finished he asked, "Did you learn it?"

"Yes," she said, "I will go now and sing it to my children." She started running as soon as she left the grasshopper. When she was halfway there a flock of pigeons was in a cornfield. As she got close, the pigeons flew in front of her. Then she fell backward. When she got up she tried to remember the song but she had forgotten it.

"I think I will go back and ask the grasshopper again. I am sure he stays there all the time. He'll probably sing for me again." She turned around and went back. When she arrived, he was still sitting at the same place as when she first left him there.

"How come you are coming back?" he asked her.

"A flock of no-good pigeons scared me on my way and I forgot the song, so I came back to ask you to sing for me again."

After he sang for her, she said, "Now I will go and sing for my children." She ran down the hill and a rodent went in front of her. She got frightened and forgot her song again. She started off by singing, "Ca-we-me, Ca-we-me," but she couldn't remember the rest of the song.

The grasshopper saw the old coyote coming in the distance. He said to himself, "This time I am getting tired, I won't sing to her." So he curled up in a ball and sat there. When the coyote got close, she said, "You help me again. A fat rodent went in front of me and I forgot my song again." She waited for him to sing for her, but he didn't say or do anything. Then she asked, "Aren't you going to sing for me?" The grasshopper sat there without saying a word. "If you won't sing for me when I ask you for the fourth time, I am going to eat you," the coyote threatened him.

She asked once, then twice, and the third and fourth time. Then she threatened him again by saying, "I am going to eat you up if you don't sing for me." The grasshopper didn't move an inch. He just sat there all curled up. Then the coyote put the grasshopper in her mouth. Just before she ate him, he turned into a rock. When she took a bite, to her surprise, the grasshopper was a rock.

That is why the coyotes have teeth that are short in front and scattered.

During that same day, a boy who lived in Hawikuh, the son of a priest, asked his father if he could go and hunt. He told his father that he was tired of staying in the house all the time. "Okay, you can go," his father told him. He went to look around the west side and heard someone singing. So he went toward where the singing was coming from. When he came near the area of the singing, the grasshopper said, "Are you going someplace?"

"Yes, where are you?" the boy asked.

"I am over here," said the grasshopper as he revealed himself. "I am singing so that my corn will ripen and it will all be ready for the harvest. You are lucky to come and see me. I have grown a lot of things and would like for someone else to look after them. Then when the time comes to plant again, you will have the seeds and they won't be wasted. You call your people together and they will help you," said the grasshopper to the boy. As soon as he was told, he returned home.

When he arrived, his father asked him, "Why are you home now?"

He answered, "On my way I heard someone singing so I went there and I found a grasshopper. He gave me all of his vegetables and everything he grew. He said he doesn't have a home to go to and that is why he would like for us to get the fruits and vegetables and use the seeds again the next time we plant them. He also said that we are to ask the people to help us so that we could get it done in one day. What shall we do? Shall we ask the people to help us or shall we do it ourselves?"

"Well," his father said, "I guess we will ask them to help us." He told his wife to go get the priest who takes messages to the people.

After he was told about the notification, he went out and told the people that they were to help the Head Priest's family work in the fields in four days.

On the day of work they all came down and helped. Some were picking beans, some picked corn and husked it, some picked melons and took them from the field. They worked until the sun went down.

"You can go now," the son said, and they went home.

He turned and went to the grasshopper. "Did you finish now?" the grasshopper asked.

"Yes," the son replied.

"Now I will stay here and what I worked hard for, I have given to you. As for me, I will eat whatever I can and I will stay in the fields. After you have distributed the seeds among the people I will also eat at the fields of other people, because they will be using the seeds that came from the fruits and vegetables," said the grasshopper.

This is what happened a long time ago and that is why the grasshopper lives in the fields and eats from the fields, because he doesn't have a home to go to.

28   A Coyote and a Bumblebee

Many years ago, there lived a bumblebee in his home among some trees. His neighbor, the coyote, lived at the coyote's pond. One day the coyotes were hunting and the bumblebee was flying around to see if he could find some pollen. The coyote came to the bumblebee and said, "Oh, my neighbor!"

"Yes," said the bumblebee.

"Are you looking for pollen?" asked the coyote.

"Yes!" the bumblebee told him. "I'm very hungry."

"Oh, well, I'm also hungry and I'm hunting for some food," said the coyote.

"I hope you find food. Well, I had better go home now. I live a long way from here," said the bumblebee.

"Where do you live?" asked the coyote.

"I think I told you, at the place of many thorns. You must come over tomorrow," the bumblebee said to the coyote.

"I will," said the coyote.

They separated and went to their own homes. Then the next morning the coyote told his family, "I have made friends with the bumblebee and he asked me to come over, so I am going today."

He went out of his house and started off in the direction of the bumblebee's house. When he arrived there, there were a lot of bumblebees sitting around.

"Are you just now coming?" asked the bumblebee.

"Yes," the coyote replied.

"Then let us all go inside," said the bumblebee.

When they got inside they talked for a while. Then the bumblebee took a bowl and said, "Now, little ones, go up to the roof and jump on it." So the little bees all got up and went up to the roof. They began to jump on it. When they jumped, pollen fell from the roof into the bowl. The bumblebee took the pollen and shaped it into little balls which he gave to all of the bumblebees, and also the coyote. They ate the yellow pollen and the coyote found it to be very tasty and good. After a while, the coyote said it was time for him to leave.

"I'd better go now," he said. "Will you come over to my house tomorrow?" he asked the bumblebee. With that, the coyote left.

The next morning the bumblebee said, "I had better go and see what the coyote will do to impress me." He went out and soon he was at the coyote's house. The coyotes all welcomed him. They were sitting outside of the cave.

"Oh, we are so glad that you could come." They visited for a while, then as the bumblebee had told his little ones to jump on the roof, so the coyote instructed his little coyotes to do the same. He held a bowl under the roof. But when the little coyotes jumped on the roof, nothing fell into the bowl but dust. From this he formed a ball and gave a piece to each coyote and the bumblebee. Then they all sat down to eat it, and pretended it tasted good. The bumblebee tasted it and found it tasted hot, but he pretended that it was good. They visited some more, then the bumblebee decided it was time to leave. He invited the coyote to come and see him the following day. The coyote agreed.

The next day, the coyote journeyed to the bumblebee's house once more. When he arrived there they greeted him.

"We're very glad you could come. Now shall we all go inside?" they said.

The coyote followed the bees into their hive. Then the bumblebee said, "Let us smoke for a while." He put a corn husk down and he fixed his tobacco so he could smoke it. He looked toward the coyote to see if he was finished. The coyote was finished, but as he looked toward the fireplace, there were no coals in it. The bumblebee held out his antenna and said, "I'll light your tobacco for you with this."

After the bumblebee lit his tobacco, they talked some more. Then the coyote said he was going to return home. He again asked the bumblebee to come to his house the following day. The bumblebee once more agreed.

On his way home, the coyote took some bark off the trees. He went home with these pieces of bark. He made them into bunches and twisted them so they would pick fire easily.

"I will leave for the coyote's house now," said the bumblebee. When he arrived at the coyote's house, they greeted him warmly, and suggested they all go inside. Before the bumblebee entered the house the little coyotes had put bark in their father's ears. These they lit and then their father went out to meet the bumblebee. When they entered the cave, the coyote suggested that they smoke. So the little coyotes were busy getting tobacco and leaves. The bumblebee finished rolling his tobacco first and needed a light. The coyote then put his ears out and said, "Why don't you light your tobacco right here?"

The bumblebee laughed when he saw smoke coming from the coyote's ears. After they had lit their cigarettes, they sat and talked some more. Soon, the bumblebee said he was sorry but he had to leave.

But a long time before this, the coyote was wishing that the bumblebee would leave, because the bark was very small and it was beginning to burn his ears. But the bumblebee talked on and on. Then finally, the bumblebee said he was leaving, so the coyote readily agreed without hesitating. By the time the little ones took the bark out of the coyote's ears, the ears of the coyote were all burned and charred. That is why the coyotes have burned ears.

The next morning the coyote went to the bumblebee's house once again. They were all sitting outside the house. They greeted him, as usually was the case. He joined them and they talked for a while. Then the bumblebee told the little ones to get him a bow and some arrows. When these were brought to him he struck a rock and it turned into a deer. This they skinned and they all ate a piece of it. When the coyote was ready to leave, he again invited the bumblebee to visit him. The bumblebee agreed. So the next day the bumblebee went to the house of the coyote.

They all greeted him and he joined them, for they were all sitting on the outside of the cave. They visited for a while, then the little ones said they were hungry. So the coyote told them to bring him his bow and some arrows. They brought the bow and arrows to him, and he aimed at a rock. As the arrow hit the rock, he instructed them to all go skin it. But the arrow bounded off the rock and killed all of the coyotes.

The bumblebee was very sorry for the coyote and his family. He got up and returned home. When he got there, the bees were all waiting to hear what foolish trick the coyote had tried this time. The bumblebee told them that the coyotes were all dead. He said it was not wise to copy someone else, if you did not have the powers to do so. He said he hoped all the bumblebees had learned a good lesson from this happening.

This is what happened a long time ago, as told to us by our ancestors.

V RELIGION

29   The Beginning

The time arrived that the stars were told by the Great Spirit to come down into the fourth womb where the people lived, giving offerings of corn pollen to their fathers.

There were always many people upon the face of the earth, but few of them were desirable. The people of the fourth womb would be brought up to stabilize what life was to be like on the surface.

Down into the darkness of the fourth womb, the stars entered where they were greeted by some hunter.

Asked who they were and what they were doing, they claimed to be the Ahauda. They came into the Gyaatdoweh's house and exclaimed that the sun wished their presence upon the earth. But first the Gyaatdoweh asked each different society to give their opinions on the question put forth to them. The Gyaatdonneh and Chuatdonneh discussed the subject and decided on the certain plants with which they were to come to the surface. As each different plant was grown for them to ascend upon, each plant failed. From the yucca roots to the thin willows were planted as each of the fourth levels of the wombs came up. Finally they penetrated onto the surface of the earth.

The Shewanaquelo and Clown clans were the first of any medicinal societies taken into the light of the sun. When they were upon the surface, they were stood facing the east from which the sun rose.

Instructed to keep their eyes opened and looking at the sun, they stood squinting at the brightness of the light surrounding them, their eyes watering. They stood until their eyes got accustomed to the light.

When these people emerged onto the surface, the strong sacred scent of the wombs that penetrated onto the surface killed the living on the face of the earth. A new group of beings began the start of a new people.

A short time later there came tremors from the underground and when that was stilled, the stars entered back into the womb, asking whom they had left behind.

Indeed, there in the opening in the fourth womb, the Coyote Clan stood halfway out of the womb exclaiming that it had been left behind and so now was coming up to join in the making of the new world, telling of its usefulness and that its members were beings from the grain of the wheat.

The Coyote Clan was led to join with the rest of the clans that had already ascended onto the earth.

There were no more tremors for a short time. But when there were, the Ahauda quickly checked the emerging point of the people from below.

They came to find one from the witch society, already sitting upon the earth with an ear of yellow corn held tightly in his hand. He claimed the usefulness of his purpose, being closely related to the Gyaatdoweh and Chuatdoweh. But at this the Ahauda went back to the rest of the clans inquiring the validity of the statements made by this person.

"Uhmdehseh," meaning a witch, has come among the people.

As there had been no previous deeds of the witch that could make him undesirable, the clans agreed to accept him into the part of a society being formed.

So the Ahauda brought the witch and he gave one ear

of corn to each clan as a gesture of friendliness. When no more emerged, the journey to find their homes started. For four years they came, with the head priest leading them to their place of settling.

As the leader scouting ahead became tired, another took the lead, going until all had led their people, leaving only the son and daughter of a high priest. Then these two walked on ahead of their people until their followers were behind and out of sight. The girl was tired, so she sat beside a sagebrush to wait for her people to catch up with them. Her brother kept going until he found what he was looking for. Then he returned to the place where he had left his sister. He found her sleeping and stood a moment looking at her, until he had lost his senses and committed incest with his sister. When that had been done the sin they had committed turned them into Mudheads, the boy being the father and the girl being the mother of nine Mudheads later produced.

Their people came upon them and, although shocked, they accepted it as a sign of how their lives were to be shaped thereafter.

Indeed, when the two became Mudheads, at that same place there appeared water and made a spring with the river streaming down into the valley. There in the valley they produced two hills rising about where the spirits of the Mudheads dwell in one and the Kachinas in the other.

They summoned their people to follow farther. As the people crossed the stream with their children on their backs, once they stepped into the stream the children became small animals, getting off their parents' backs and going into the water.

There the people who had crossed had been split in half, with their children turning into aquatic species.

The leaders advised the rest to stay ashore on the opposite side of the river until they could figure some other way to go over without losing their children to the water. When they could not come up with a way, they advised the people to come across but to hold tightly to their children until they had crossed to the other bank.

Once more the people came into the river, their children turning into fishes, frogs, turtles, and other aquatic species. Their hold on the children was tight, and no one was lost. As they stepped onto the opposite bank the children became themselves as they had been before.

When they all had crossed, the children lost to the river went into the small water hole where the father of the Mudheads and their mother founded as their home "Koh-thlou-wah-la-wah."

As new leaders were chosen, they kept coming until dusk when the chanting of the spirits of masked dancers was heard.

The priests were sent back to Koh-thlou-wah-la-wah to find what had taken place. They entered the small water hole where they found the lost children, who had been turned into Kachinas.

The two priests were assured that the children who had stayed at Koh-thlou-wah-la-wah were happy and assured them to tell their parents not to think about them any longer.

The priests returned to their people with the news and related the previous night's happenings.

Again they started on their journey. Each time they stopped four years at a place until they moved farther on. When they came to Honthlebinkyn they stopped for another four years. The Gyaatdonneh's brother and Chuatdonneh's sister announced that they could no longer stay with the same clan and that they must go where great bodies of water lay.

So the people again split after four years. The priests set a period of ritual in offering the blessings to the spirits of their children in Koh-thlou-wah-la-wah. During the four high priests' time, the dates of rituals were in the days when daily showers came, making the grounds rich and fertile.

When the rains fell, as the rivers came rushing down where the water frothed about, the two Ahauda came into view. Thus far they had been seen as the stars that first brought the people upon their emerging. When that happened, the sun priests came forth and the Ahauda now stayed with their people while the stars went back up into the skies.

The Ahauda stayed peacefully for only a short time; then they started to roam about the land where later they killed a Cheskekchkkya.

This girl didn't die, and later on regained consciousness, starting to follow the two Ahauda.

The two fled into Shebabulima where they entered into clans and societies seeking safety and refuge from the girl. But no one came to their assistance until finally they came to the Knife Clan.

The clan took them in and assured them safety. First they were prepared in the dress of the Bow Priests and given little bundles of sticks, then told to sit in a corner facing the entrance.

The girl came bounding onto the roof and spoke into the house asking if the two were in there. When she was told they were, she asked for them to be sent out but was refused. Instead she was told to come in and get them if she wanted them.

She came on down the ladder. About the time she stepped on the third rung the two cried out in terror, then mocked her appearance, which made her run back up onto the roof.

She tried two more times but ran back out. Angered and humiliated, she went down for the fourth time, determined to get the two War Gods.

The War Gods continued to mock her until as soon as she set her foot on the floor they attacked, striking her with the sticks until she fell in a lifeless heap.

The leader of the Knife Clan instructed them to take her scalp, and when they had done so, further instructions were given to them.

They were to tie the scalp to the end of a long thin post with a twig of sagebrush, then to stand the post outside the house. Then they were told to dispose of the lady in any way and anywhere they wanted, so the two War Gods took the body out and not very far from the house they left it out in the sun and returned to the clan house.

When they came in they found the tracks of a bird, some looking as if it was entering and some as if going out. The two argued for a moment as to the direction the tracks were going, and shortly the leader asked them to check behind the altar to see if there was anything there. They checked and found the bird sitting in a corner behind the altar. They were told to count the feathers on the wings, and they found twelve on each. The priests of the clan then set the fasting days to twelve days, during which time they would be saved and blessings would be asked for them.

When the period was over, they were sent to the Gyaatdoweh's house. They were taught the songs for the Scalp Dance and were instructed to go into the village and as they circled it to sing the scalping songs.

When they did as they were told, the people came out and joined the procession around the village four times. Then they entered the plaza where the scalps were in the center. Four days later, night dancing started after the scalp was washed.

When the four nights of dancing were finished, the War Gods were set out in the plaza with the pollen and grains of wheat while the dancing went on all day.

When this day ended, the monster from below, the tornado and the rest of the terrible things, came up from the fourth womb. Along with those things came a coyote possessing supernatural powers who was summoned to start the dances for the purification rites; when once again they rose to come looking for the middle place.

The War Gods came into Halona and settled there until the Bow Priests found themselves to be relieved of their play by some other group. They called a session among the leaders of the people and discussed the news.

"We will be shortly taken to a place for us, we must all go. But there are some of us unwilling to accept the destiny we are headed for. We have lived with a feeling of well-being and desire to continue; should we be dissolved to nothing so easily?

"No, we have taken care of our land, letting it flourish and nurturing it. We do not wish to be set aside without struggle."

The situation was discussed and it was agreed that the dams and banks be broken, so the bodies of water could meet, forming one great lake. All the land was to be covered with water and when it became dry, the ground would solidify, becoming stable, and no more threats of being destroyed would come.

The next day the prayersticks were prepared and planted in the rivers, streams, lakes, ponds, and anywhere that water was. When they did that, the water became great bodies, and the people fled to the top of Towayalane where they settled in small villages until the rising waters subsided. After many years the water dried out and the land became hard and solid. While the water came into the land there came a large serpent from the oceans, which later as the water lowered cried out from behind the south mountain. From then on the mountains were known as the Face Mountain.

Before the land dried out, the priests decided to ask the priest's children to enter the bodies of water, where they would meet the supernatural and where they would ask for the salvation of their people.

When a boy and a girl agreed to go, the preparations began. The prayersticks were placed in baskets with pollen. Then the children were painted with sacred paints and feathers were placed in their mouths, hair, and arms.

The day passed, and early next morning they were led along a path where people stood along the sides praying for them and encouraging them. When they reached the edge of the cliff, their brothers and sisters came up to them for the last time, assuring them that they would never die and that they should live among their brothers and sisters, parents and grandparents forever.

As they walked into the waters, the great bodies stilled. As silence came and the two reached the floors of the water, the water began to lower, and the surrounding things along the water's edge turned into rocks, also turning the boy and girl into stones. The water slowly went into the ground and many years passed and finally the ground became hard.

The two stones along the west of the mountains are believed to be the priest's children. When the people came down upon the dry, hard ground, they found the tracks of two people going all the way to Koh-thlou-wah-la-wah.

When the people came back down into their village, they once more settled for only a short time, when the priests asked each other if Halona was really the middle place.

The worm was summoned and asked to use his supernatural

powers to indicate if Halona was the middle place. When the priests were assured that it was, they still wanted further assurances. They called upon the water spider to find the middle place. The water spider came from the north and it stretched its legs until its body lay upon the center. Then upon that exact spot the village was built. Under the houses where the priests now spend their fasting days, there lies the heart of the earth, the middle place.

30 Two Girls and the Dancers

In Matsakya many years ago when the supernatural beings, our ancestors, came from Koh-thlou-wah-la-wah as Kachinas, they danced during a feast as spectators gathered around to watch them. The Kachinas were the Rain Dancers and in the group there were two who danced without the Kachina masks. They were handsome as they performed.

When through with their dance, they started to file out of the plaza. Near the entrance to the plaza were two girls who watched them very closely. As the last of them went out, the girls came behind them. The Kachinas were now on their way to Koh-thlou-wah-la-wah when they saw the girls behind them and asked, "Do you want to come with us?"

"Yes, we do."

"If you wish to come, then we will take you along."

When they reached Koh-thlou-wah-la-wah, the Kachinas entered their home and the girls followed. They came to sit against the wall. The Kachinas that had been left there were dancing when the Rain Dancers told the rest about the two girls they had brought back with them.

"If they wish to stay here, there are no objections from us." So the girls stayed with the Kachinas and were well cared for. The girls' only reason for coming to Koh-thlou-wah-la-wah was the two young men who had impressed them during the dances.

As time passed, the Kachinas approached them and told them, "Our children, we think it will be better if you return to your own land. We do not think it will be for the best if you continue to stay here among us. You have still a long life-span before you. You should not have come here, but you did."

They answered, "It is because of the two young men that we came along."

"But you still should not have come. Look," the leader turned to a line sprinkled with cornmeal, which shone long and clear. "Your life is young and you have far yet to go."

With the long lines were many more, varied in length, some very short and others lengthy.

They were told "The lines indicate your life-span. The short ones are the newborn who failed to survive and have come amongst us. As you have seen, you have a long time left before you will be back."

"So it is."

"You two will only look at us and remember well what you have seen. You will return to your people and tell them of what you have seen and of how we live. We will no longer come into the villages, for more might wish to come with us only to return later to their people."

"So it shall be."

"Indeed, for we have spoken. Now you will observe us closely and memorize what you are to see. You will observe and take in every detail of each dance we perform for you."

The next day, the Kachinas spoke to them, "We will take you home now." They brought the two girls to the outskirts of the village and the Kachinas returned to Koh-thlou-wah-la-wah.

The two girls came on home where they were greeted and asked, "So you have come back?"

"Yes, we are here."

"Did our ancestors, the Kachinas who danced, take you with them?"

"Yes, for we saw and were moved by the two young men who danced without the shield of the Kachina masks. We were taken and shown the spirits of the ones we have lost. They danced nightly and we were shown what you will create. You will make the replicas of the dancers you have seen and from now on we will preserve them; the supernatural ones will come by breath in the winds and join us. When the dancing stops, they alone will return to Koh-thlou-wah-la-wah and that way, the lives of our people will remain on this land until their time comes. We were sent back because we have a long time to go before we can join our ancestors. Each of us has her own destiny and life-span. You will make the beings on which we will be dependent for the blessings of rain and beauty. Once they have been prepared, they will be with us forever in spirit."

So it was at that time the Kachinas of today were created from the detailed descriptions of the two girls. From that time on, the people asked for blessings with prayer and rituals carried out by the Kachina cult.

With the creation of dancers came the initiation of young

boys, for in order to participate one had to be formally inducted into one of the six Kachina cults.

In order to be fully initiated, one has to go through two rituals of flogging. The first ritual, which takes place in the plaza, prepares the young boys for the second flogging, which is done in the secrecy of the main kiva where the final binding rituals are carried out

It is from the words of our ancestors we bring back what they dictated. In these times of discontent and warfare, for those of us who believe in the ways of our people and their belief in the spirits of the supernatural, we believe we are protected against the visible weapons of our enemies, no matter what the form or substance. The beliefs sustain us through danger, slight or crucial. The spirits come out against our enemies before our destruction and prepare us with the strength and tolerance essential for the spirit to live through life.

And so we have come this far in life and we look forward to the future.

31   True Way of the Scalp Dance

When our village came to being, the times were hard as the land was yet untamed. The people knew the ways of their ancestors and practiced them going about the rituals without hesitating or relying upon others.

Such was the ritual of the Scalp Dance. A man knew within himself of his capabilities, his purposes and obligations;

without so much as a word the man would set a time in his mind and proceed to execute what he made up his mind to do. He would go out alone, prepared for his undertaking, whether it would be right away or sometime in the future. So we were brought up with this knowledge and in my younger days when I participated in many rituals, I knew by instinct when a scalping would take place and what would follow. But the rituals would be kept in secrecy, especially when the Ahauda were involved, for they were a law unto the rituals.

Chants and prayers were the ways in which we expressed our feelings. Although the Ahauda were the most sacred in this particular ritual, and the most feared for their destructive ways because scalping was of their commands, the Ahauda were dear.

When a scalp was being brought into the village, the people awakened early in the morning and blessed themselves with the spirits of the dead brought to them by the breezes. Shortly, the procession was headed, led there by female relatives of the priests-to-be, to circle the village slaughtering horses, dogs, and other strays. However, it seems the people today who take part in these rituals deliberately delay the proceedings, therefore prolonging and in the process eliminating certain phases of the rituals.

The Ant Clan, the Batdonneh, and the Bow Priests who had such a ritual long ago, revealed to us that they had forgotten some details of the ceremonies. That seems incredible because from generation to generation our forefathers, no matter how much the length of time that passed between such rituals, whether one year or five years, never failed to display an event, showing such negligence. As many times as the Scalp Dance has been repeated, what causes the sudden lapse into forgetfulness?

A short time ago, when the ritual was once more partaken, each one of the priests-to-be balked and hesitated so as to delay for such a length of time that it was considered totally alien to the old ways. While in the days long ago, though problems at that time seemed impossible, the rituals were always carried on without a moment's delay and the dances were completed.

Our young people tend to take their time in doing anything today: then it was supposed that if a ritual was done in only the length of time necessary, the blessings given us would have the power of youth and vigor everlasting.

The Scalp Dance that took place not long ago neglected a number of important aspects of the ritual, such as the feather of the roadrunner worn by the initiates. Though I do not know exactly why the feather is important, I was told only a few words of its being. It is known that for some reason the Ant Clan saved the Ahauda when the brothers were asked to guess at what the roadrunner had done, whether it entered a small burrow or whether the tracks were leading away from the burrow. The older of the Ahauda was asked first for his answer, and he answered that the roadrunner had gone out of the burrow, while his little brother answered that the roadrunner had gone in. There they were instructed to do what was going to be and then taken into the Knife Society. There the younger of the two was initiated into the Kachina cult, and the other only blessed so he would have the strength and courage for endurance and tolerance.

Because this happened, the Ant Clan members became their parents, so that when the Ahauda were prepared they were dressed the way they are, and the chants, prayers, and songs sung to them are theirs alone.

But again, because of the delay in the ceremonies today, the last time this happened the songs were not completed while the ritual of painting the Bow Priests was being done. As each garment is adorned upon them, prayers are said and chanted and songs sung. Until this has been done, the Bow Priests do not come after the scalps, but again, because of their negligence, these rituals have been somewhat altered. That on the morning, the last morning when the completion of the rituals takes place, each head of each ritual is to be adorned with the feathers that depict the greatness of natural elements.

For some time these rituals, even some social ceremonies, were almost abolished by the influence of the Spaniards, but as the ceremonies once more began to take place, the old people like me began to function as the leaders of the societies. And because we have kept our knowledge and preserved our ways, we have been kept in our posts of leadership, for rarely does a young person wish the knowledge we have to himself. One does not learn by keeping silent for I too had to inquire of many persons, some who no longer are among us, people like Hoonki who had learned from his father the true forms of expressing what we believed in.

Some of us who remember what we have been told, especially about these rituals, wonder why it is we have intermingled with those who were considered our enemies. For now, our young people have intermingled with members of tribes we once warred against. These situations were feared and condemned many years ago and now we wonder if time has changed the way of the spirits, for we have been shown what could and might have happened. The blessings that we ask for ourselves are shown throughout the last phase of the ceremony when we offer arrows three times and the last when we give an offering of material value. These have come to being as they are now only through the efforts of a few who truly believe in the old ways and the spirits of our ancestors.

32 Matsakya

At Matsakya village, there were these two Yahahnas. Every night in the village from one of the kivas, there were children playing and wrestling in there. These Yahahnas would watch them disapprovingly.

One night, they went home to Koh-thlou-wah-la-wah and told the spirits of our ancestors what the children were doing in their homes, the kivas. The Yahahnas wanted to punish the children and since they were going to be back through on their way to Matsakya they wanted to see what their ancestors thought should be done.

The next morning, the two Yahahnas washed up, and in the evening they had their hair combed and got all dressed up and painted. These handsome Yahahnas were ready to leave when the leaders gave them some instructions.

A cigarette was made and the Yahahnas were told to go to the kiva, leave the cigarette, and indicate, by marking four lines with some sacred cornmeal on the floor of the kiva, that in four days something would happen. By doing this, they thought the children would get the idea that something evil would happen to them if they kept playing in the kivas.

They waited to enter the village at night when the children started having fun. They came into the kiva by going down a ladder and when they went back to the top, they threw some of their sacred cornmeal in the doorway. The children did not hear them come, although one of them saw the Yahahnas coming and gave a warning to the others; but they were having fun and did not notice. Then they saw the cornmeal and the Yahahnas come in, and the children were scared stiff and immobilized.

Then one of the older children regained his sense, ran over to a house where an old man lived, and told him of what had happened. The man put on his shawl and told the child, "This was what you have been asking for, playing in the kivas."

When they reached the kiva, the man came on it, picked up the cigarette, and blessed the Yahahnas with the sacred cornmeal. He made a prayer and the Yahahnas left, going back to Koh-thlou-wah-la-wah. After the four days had passed, the spirits of the ancestors put on their costumes for the dance they were going to do in the kiva. One of them did not wear his mask but painted himself with black powder. Before they left, they danced at home, singing a song saying that they were going to Matsakya to get two ladies.

At Matsakya, the people gathered in the kiva to watch the dance. During the night, two girls went outside to wait for them at the rooftop of the kiva, where the opening led to the outside.

As the ancestors were leaving, one of the girls caught this man that was not wearing his mask, telling him she was going with them. At first he refused to take her, but she insisted on going along. So the man carried the girl on his back, telling her to keep her eyes closed all the way until they got to Koh-thlou-wah-la-wah. Then the Kachinas transformed themselves into birds and away they flew.

When they reached their destination, they told her of their reason for their visit to Matsakya. Since the people did not know what to do, she was to go home and tell the elders of what they were to do for their ancestors. So the next day, she went back home to tell her people that whenever two of their ancestors came to the village, marking the ground with cornmeal, this meant that the spirits were to come in four days and perform a dance. The people should then cook food and feed the spirits. Also, they should make a cigarette and have the two that came smoke it and pray to the spirits so that they could bestow upon the people a good life in the future.

When she was through, she told them that she had to return to Koh-thlou-wah-la-wah for eternity, that she was the one taken as a sacrifice for all the harm the children had done in the kivas. Four days passed by and the girl died. Her spirit entered into Koh-thlou-wah-la-wah, as were the spirits of our ancestors and will be the spirits of our people who pass on.

33 Priest's Son and the Spirit World

A long time ago in Kyakima, there lived a priest and his son. The priest's son was a very good deer hunter and every day he would bring home to his father a deer.

East from their house there lived another priest and his daughters and sons. The oldest of the priest's daughters was always thinking about this famous deer hunter. Then one day she put on her best clothes and got her water jug and went down to the well to get some water. Here she waited for the deer hunter to pass by. When he arrived she greeted him, "Oh, there you are."

"Yes, I am here," said the deer hunter.

The girl demanded, "You will go and kill me the biggest deer you can kill."

"I will try," said the hunter.

"After you have brought me the deer, we shall get married,"

said the girl. The hunter did not like the idea of getting married so he replied, "I'll kill you the deer but I don't want to get married because when we get married I don't want you in the way of my thinking. I won't be able to be a good hunter after we are married." With this said he went off to his hunting grounds and before long he killed a great big deer. He cut his deer's stomach and got the insides out. On the ground, he put the sacred cornmeal and placed the insides of the deer. Since it was still too early to return he waited until just past noon. The deer was dry just a little so the hunter put the deer on his back and returned to the village. As he neared the village the girl was waiting for the hunter. She greeted him as before, "Oh, here you are."

"Yes, I'm back," said the hunter. The hunter didn't stop but just kept on walking toward his house. The girl was so disappointed that she just turned and went home. The hunter was expecting the girl to say, "Oh, here you are. Thank you very much for killing the deer."

When the girl got home her parents asked her, "Did he give you the deer?"

"No, he didn't give me the deer."

"That's what we thought," said her parents. "You were supposed to have said, 'Oh, here you are, thank you very much for killing the deer for me.' But you didn't say that," said the parents.

"I will try again tomorrow," said the girl.

The next day she met the hunter at the well and she asked the hunter to kill a deer for her. The hunter said, "I will try and kill a deer for you. However, you will wait and wish for it."

He went off to the same place where he was the day before. Before long he killed another big deer and waited until after the deer had dried a little. It was past noon when he started home with his deer. The girl was sitting for him at the same place. As he came closer she greeted him as before.

"Oh, here you are."

"Yes, I'm back," said the hunter. He didn't stop since the girl didn't greet him with "Thank you very much for the deer." The girl went home to her parents without the deer. When she got there her parents asked, "Did you get the deer?"

"No, I didn't get the deer. That hunter, I have asked him to kill me a deer and for two days he has killed the deer I wanted but he hasn't given them to me," said the girl.

Since the girl didn't get the deer she was heartbroken and her feelings were hurt. The girl was bad and evil. She was a witch and, being a witch, she planned on getting even with the deer hunter who was supposed to have brought her the deer.

That evening the girl turned to her brother and asked him, "Will you do me a favor?"

The brother answered, "What would you like for me to do?" Then his sister told him that she wanted the hunter killed.

The brother asked, "What will I use to kill the hunter?"

The girl told her brother, "The weapon will be the thing that he is thinking and hunting, and that is the deer. You will go to his hunting grounds and along the path you will walk toward the east, and you will turn yourself into a deer and you will then have deer tracks. You will wait for the hunter in the nearby bushes. When the hunter comes toward you, you will run toward him and kill him with your horns."

"If that is the way you want me to kill the deer hunter, I will do my best," said the brother.

When the girl was telling her plan to her brother, the deer hunter's friend was present to hear the plan. "Well, I guess I better be going home," said the friend. The friend went to his house but he didn't go in, but instead he went over to the deer hunter's house to visit him. The friend was concerned about the hunter's life and he just had to go to warn his friend.

When the friend got to the hunter's house, he said "Good evening." The deer hunter was surprised because his friend never came to visit them.

"What brings you to our house? What have you to say?" asked the hunter.

"My brother, I am worried about you. The girl who asked you to kill the deer for her has gotten her feelings hurt and she is heartbroken and wants to get even with you. Tomorrow her brother will try to kill you by turning himself into a deer."

"Is this what you have heard?" asked the hunter.

"Yes, and this is what you will do," said the friend. "You will go to your hunting grounds like you always do. Along the path, you will see the footprints and along the top of the mountain you will find that the prints will turn west and then the prints will turn to deer tracks. I want to help you. Give me two of your arrows."

The hunter's friend went home and fixed the arrows. He removed the arrowheads and placed the bee pollen inside the arrowheads. Then he took the two arrows back to the hunter's house and told him how to use the arrows. The friend told the hunter that the bee pollen would turn to bees when the hunter shot the arrow into the deer's head.

"Very well," said the hunter.

That night the hunter didn't sleep well. He kept thinking about what his friend had told him of the girl's plan. Just before the sun came up the hunter went out to ask for the blessings from our Father, the Sun. When he came back to the house his wife had prepared his breakfast. After his meal, his wife gave him his lunch in a bag and his bow and arrows. And the hunter turned to his wife and said, "Well, I guess I'll be going. We'll see what kind of day I'll have today." Then he started off to his hunting grounds.

As he was leaving the village the girl saw him leave and she thought to herself, "Well, there you go. You'll be happy and gay just for a little while and in a short time you will meet your death."

The hunter went along the path and saw the footprints his friend had told him about. At the top of the mountain the prints turned west a little way and then the deer tracks appeared and went toward the east. Finally he came face to face with a big deer. He thought to himself, "Well, this must be the deer my friend told me about." Then the deer ran toward the hunter, but the hunter shot the arrow into the deer's head. The bees came out and stung the deer's eyes out, and the deer fell dead. The hunter then turned and went south to roam until late in the afternoon. He went back home without the deer.

In the village the girl was waiting for her brother to return. Darkness came and her brother hadn't come back. The girl thought to herself, "Well, I guess you have met your enemy and you have lost your life."

The friend was there visiting the girl. The girl then turned to her younger brother to do her a favor. She said, "We must kill the hunter. I ask you, my brother, to kill him for me."

The brother asked, "What will I use as a weapon?"

The girl said, "Tomorrow, you will become a bear, because no one has ever killed a bear. East from here is a mountain called the Corn Mountain and there you will wait for the hunter."

Her younger brother said, "On the south side next to the big rock I will wait and as soon as the hunter comes up, I will grab the hunter and tear him limb from limb."

The deer hunter's friend was there again to hear her plan. It was getting late, so the friend said, "Shall we get some rest, because when we get a good night's rest, we'll be able to kill the hunter."

The friend left for his house but instead he went to his friend's house to tell him about the girl's plan. The friend told the hunter, "There will be footprints along the path and then, at the top of Corn Mountain, the footprints will change to bear tracks. You will follow the tracks and you will use the arrow I prepared for you."

"That I will do," said the hunter.

The next day the hunter took his bow and arrows and went off to hunt the bear. He found the prints along the path and followed them to the top of the Corn Mountain, where the prints changed to bear tracks. Before the hunter knew it he saw the bear. The hunter shot the last arrow into the bear's eyes and the pollen turned into bees. The bees stung and ate the bear's eyes out and the bear died.

The hunter walked around the forest until it was time to go home. Just before the sun went down, the hunter returned home without the bear.

The hunter's friend was at the girl's house again, visiting as before.

The girl waited again for her brother. It was late at night when she said to herself, "I guess you have lost your life." She turned to her younger sister to seek help to kill the hunter. The younger sister was willing to try and she agreed to help her sister.

The younger sister asked, "What will I use as a weapon to kill the hunter?" Then the deer hunter's friend spoke up, "Oh, please, let us give up this killing and put a stop to it. You have already lost two of your brothers. It is very hard to kill a deer hunter because he was given sacred cornmeal to give him strength against his enemies."

The girl said, "I'm not going to give up, because the hunter promised me the two deer but he didn't give those two deer. The weapon you will use is an insect called siyayaka [gnat].

"Tomorrow the hunter will go to his cornfield instead of going hunting. The sun will be so hot that the gnats will surround him," said the girl. Then she turned to her sister and said, "As the gnats surround him, you will come as a gnat and give him his first warning. Then you come around to his left ear and there you will go inside his ear. Inside the ear, you will shout and yell. From there, you will go to his brain and you will eat his brains and he will die quickly."

"Okay," said the little sister.

The friend suggested that they get some sleep since it was getting late. The friend left for his house but when he saw that the hunter was still up, the friend decided to go visit him and tell him about this other plan. The hunter was waiting for his friend. He greeted his friend. "Oh, you have come. Come in and sit down, and tell me what you have heard," said the hunter.

The friend said, "I do have something to tell you. Tomorrow you will go to your field since you haven't gotten a deer. When you get to your field, the sun will shine and it will be so hot that the gnats will surround you and sting you. Then the gnat who will try to kill you will come last. The gnat will go around your face and then to your left ear. The gnat will go inside your ear and as soon as the gnat goes in you will close your ear with this cotton I have brought you."

"Okay," said the hunter.

"As soon as you close the left ear, come to me. I will wait for you at your house," said his friend. With that said the friend went home.

Next day the hunter went to his field and when he got there his crops were dying from lack of water. The hunter wasn't too happy.

"What has happened to my crops? I didn't know that you are lacking water. Your heads are roasted and your hands are burned," said the hunter, talking to his crops. He walked around the field for a while and then started to hoe. The gnats came and stung him. He started scratching and scratching. The last gnat that came went around the hunter's face and gave him the warning. Then the gnat went around to the hunter's left ear and went inside. The hunter closed his ear with the cotton and ran home to his friend.

"You're back. Did you bring what I asked for?" asked his friend.

"Yes, I did," said the hunter. The hunter sat down and the friend looked inside the hunter's ear and saw the legs of the little girl who had turned into a gnat. The friend took the girl and sat her down.

"Now," said the friend, "Our grandfather who is old and has been lonely all his life will have a girl who can look after him. Our grandfather will have someone to talk to now.

"Our dear father, come out from the house and get this girl," said the friend.

This old man, a roll of cotton, made a sound from the fourth world underground. He made this sound four times and then he came up.

"My children, how are you today?" said the old man.

"Fine, thank you. So you have come up," said the friend and the hunter.

"Yes, I have come up. What do you want of me?" asked the old man.

"Very well. Look at this girl. This girl was supposed to

have eaten the hunter's brains. You will take this girl back to your fourth world underground and she will look after you," said the friend.

"So be it. Thank you very much," said the old man. The old man took the little girl and went back to where he came from. So the little girl was lost from the world. The girl waited for her little sister but she didn't come home.

The hunter didn't go back to his field that day, but the next day the hunter returned to his field and the sun was very hot. He looked around the field and saw that the crops were dried up. He turned around and went back to his house.

He talked to his father, "Father, today you will prepare me some prayersticks. After you have finished I will go and ask for rain for my crops. I will go way up high into the next kingdom in the skies where our fathers and mothers are. I will give them the prayersticks and in return they should rain for my crops."

"Very well, I will do that for you," said his father.

In the meantime, the girl gathered her other brothers and told them, "Now, my brothers, our two brothers and our little sister are dead. Tomorrow you will get even for me. I shall go way up in the skies to our fathers who will make the rain and ask for rain. My brothers, you will follow the hunter by a bird, a swallow. You will follow him to the end of the next kingdom. There you will shut the gates before he goes through. Then you will hit him with the garment and he will turn into a swallow. When he turns into a bird he will not be able to return to the earth. This is the way you will kill the hunter," said the girl.

After the brothers heard their sister give them their orders, they went to bed for a night's rest.

The next day the friend went to visit the hunter. The friend told the hunter about the girl's plan. The friend said, "When you go to your fathers to ask for rain, the girl's brothers will follow you to the gate, there they will shut you off. They will hit you with the garment and you will turn into a bird [ahahkya]. After you have turned into a bird you will not be able to come back to earth and they in turn will own all the rain kingdom."

"So that's what you have heard. So be it," said the hunter.

"Tomorrow you will go to your field and stand where you had started to plant corn. There you will turn west and put your legs apart and tell your father, the Yellow Tornado, who lives in the fourth womb underground, 'On this day you will take me to the fathers above, since you're the only one who is strong enough to take me there.' You will then give the Yellow Tornado his sacred cornmeal. When you two pass the gates, our father, the Yellow Tornado, will not leave the gate. This will make it hard for the birds to trap you or get near the gate," said the friend.

"After you get there you will turn west to the Rain Fathers and you will plant feathers for them. They will accept these feathers and they will ask you what kind of rain you want. You will tell them that you want small raindrops instead of big raindrops since small raindrops soak in more than the big ones. You will have to hurry to return to the gate so you can get through. Now, have a good night's rest," said the friend.

The next morning the hunter ate his breakfast and when he finished he went down to his father where he was making prayersticks for him. He took them to where they had started to plant his crops and he planted the prayersticks there. He turned west and saw that the birds were circling around his fields. These were the same birds that were supposed to kill him. He then asked the Sun God, "The day has come for you to stand by us. Our father from the fourth womb underground will take us to our Rain Fathers so we can plant feathers." While saying this, he put his legs apart and stood there. The Yellow Tornado was listening to him.

"My child, why is it that you want me? I will help you," he said. With this, he made some kind of noise four times. On the fourth noise he lifted the boy up and took him to the Rain Fathers. They had passed the gates before the birds did. The birds came and were circling the gates but the tornado stayed near the gate and took watch. The hunter went on to where he was supposed to go. After doing what he was told to do, he waited for their answer.

"My dear child, you have come and planted the feathers for us and we have accepted. We will help you in whatever you want us to do," said the Rain Fathers.

"I want for you to send down small drops of rain," said the hunter. "I have more to say to you but I must get back to the gate right away."

Meanwhile the birds were still around the gate, but they couldn't get by since the tornado was so strong. When the boy got there the tornado lifted the boy again and brought the hunter back to earth. The hunter was safe at home but the birds never came back to human beings. They became birds forever. They didn't kill the hunter after all.

The friend was at the girl's house again. The girl waited for her brothers but they never returned. They didn't die but they became birds. The girl was the only one left.

"All my brothers are gone and now my little sister is dead. Tomorrow night I will kill him myself," said the girl.

The girl said, "We have tried to kill the hunter so many times in so many ways, but I no longer want to kill him. I'm going to kill his wife instead, so that he can live a poor life and will turn to me for comfort. I will kill her with sleep."

"Really," said the friend, "now let us have a good night's sleep." The friend was not happy about the plan so he went to visit the hunter.

"What have you heard this time?" asked the hunter.

"My dear sister, tomorrow night the girl will kill you with sleep. Since she did not kill my brother, she has turned to you," said the friend to the hunter's wife. "You are not strong and you are not too wise for this kind of challenge. My sister, just be patient. Tomorrow night as soon as the sun goes down, bring in a lot of wood for the fire, a can for your toilet use, a large jug of cold water, and some pillows to sit on."

Then he said to the hunter, "You will sit for a while with your wife and when you get tired you will walk around the room with your wife so she will not get sleepy. You will do this until the sun comes up.

"My dear sister, you have to be brave and patient. If you are lucky, no sleep will come to you until the sun comes up. After it comes up that will be all. You will have won your life," said the friend.

"Well, we will see how things will turn out," said the hunter and his wife. The husband was not happy about this. So they went to bed with high hopes for the next day.

The girl just couldn't wait for the sun to set the next day. Meantime, the couple was getting ready for the long night. They brought in wood, a can, their pillows, and a cold jug of water. As soon as the sun set the couple sat by the fireplace and waited. After a while they got up and he took his wife's hand and walked her around and gave her some cold water to keep her awake. They did this all night long. Finally the sun was about to come up.

"My dear, be patient. The sun is almost up. If we are lucky

you will not go to sleep," said the hunter to his wife. By this time the fire had died down. "Let me put some wood in the fire," said the hunter and led his wife to the fireplace. By then the sun was almost up. He had picked up the wood to put it in the fireplace and while doing so he let her hand go. Since he let her hand go she fell asleep, and there she lost her life. The hunter said, "My dear, why did I let your hand go?" It was too late to do anything about her life.

The parents were crying and the girl who challenged the hunter and his wife was listening to their cries. She was happy because she had killed the hunter's wife.

"Good, this is what I wanted to do to you," she said. Then she turned to her mother, "Mother, go over to her house and see if they have fixed her up. See if they are going to fix her with some precious things like her jewelry. After they have buried her we will dig her back out and we will take off what they put on her. The precious things that she had on will remain in our house forever and my life will depend on it," said the girl. The mother went over to the hunter's wife's house.

"My dear child, has she gone?" asked the mother to the parents of the dead woman. "I heard your crying and came over to be of help. I see you have already fixed her up. I guess I'd better go home."

The mother then went home to tell her daughter that the girl was already fixed and she couldn't see what she was taking to the other world.

"I bet she is taking all her precious things with her, anyway," said the girl.

The parents dug a grave for their daughter and laid her down. That same evening her husband was sitting on the roof of their house. He was not happy about losing his wife. Sitting there he could see a red light where the parents had buried his wife. The hunter thought to himself, "I wonder why that red light is coming from her grave. Is this the way you must live? I am already lonely even though the night hasn't passed yet. I want to hear your voice. I think I will go down there and see her and talk to her." He got up and went down to the graveyard where she was buried.

There was a ladder leading down into her grave and a fireplace where she was sitting with her back toward the fire and her face away from the fire. The hunter spoke to her, "My dear wife, why aren't you asleep?"

She said, "I wasn't sleepy at all. Why did you come down here?"

"I saw the light and I wanted to hear your voice, and I just couldn't sleep," said the husband.

"Why did you do this? You can't come bothering me anymore since I have turned into spirit," said the dead wife.

"But I am lonely for you and want to talk to you and that is why I am here," said the husband.

"You can't come here anymore because you are still alive and a human being," said the dead wife. "Just stand out there and I will talk to you. It is late and you must go back up to your house." So he went back to his house and watched the fire as it burned out. As the sun came up the light at the wife's grave went out. Then he went back into his house and stayed there all day since he was not happy. All he could think of was his dead wife who was another person, only a spirit.

That evening the hunter sat on the rooftop again. The light at his wife's grave was burning again.

"I think I'll go down there once more. She meant everything to me, my only reason for living. She never said any mean words to me and I never had any harsh words for her. We were happy together. That is why nature gave us all that we had hoped for and wanted. Now that she has gone, I have been very sad, since we were always happy together," said the hunter to himself and then went down to his wife's grave.

"Why did you come down here again?" asked the wife. Her back was toward the fire because she no longer existed and therefore she must face toward the darkness.

"I came because I need to hear your voice again. I am going to come in there even though you don't want me to," said the hunter.

"But you must not come over here. You must stand just where you are now since you are still living and have a long time to live. I have gone before you; because of this one bad person I am no longer with you," said his wife. Her husband came in and stood at the foot of the ladder.

"I know you want to hear my voice, but I have been here two nights and in two more days I will be going to another world to meet the spirits of my mothers and fathers. I will leave early in the morning on the fourth day. At our house my parents will bake and cook for me and will feed me toward evening. They will leave the door open a little so that I will come in by means of spirit and feed myself. After feeding myself I will leave early in the morning to meet the spirits," she said to her husband.

"Oh, I see. So you will be leaving," said the husband. "Since we were always so happy and loved each other so much, I want to go with you when you go."

"No, you can't do this, because you are still living," said the wife to her husband. But the husband kept insisting on going with his wife.

"If you really want to go with me you have to really be sure of yourself that you want to go with me. And if you do you will have to make four pairs of shoes for yourself and take them with you. You will also have to take some food to eat on the way. I will leave as soon as the sun comes up. I will take the road that leads to this world, and on this road you will follow me. But I will not be seen, so I will wear this white feather. When the feather is standing still that means I will stop to rest for the night and you will do the same," she told her husband.

"So be it," said the hunter. "I really do want to go with you, since I loved you very much."

"Very well," she said, "when we do go, I hope you will be happy and content. But it all depends," she said. "I have told you not to go since you are still alive and have a long time left to live. Since you really want to go with me, will you make those shoes I told you to make?" she asked.

"Yes, I will make those shoes," said the hunter.

"Very well, as soon as my parents feed me by burning the food, I will be leaving the following morning. You should be ready to go," said the wife.

"I will be ready and waiting," he said. And he left her grave. All this time the hunter had been talking to his dead wife, he had stood at the foot of the ladder inside the grave. She had told him not to come to where she was sitting because he was still alive.

The next day the hunter got the biggest deer hide that he had killed and started making his four pairs of shoes. While he was doing this the girl's parents were cooking for her to feed her by burning the food. As soon as the sun set they opened the door and put the food in the fireplace for their dead daughter. That night the hunter prepared for his long journey. He packed the dried deer meat and paper bread. Just before the sun came up he took the pack and the shoes he had made and left the house. He came to this place that his wife had told him about and, sure enough, he saw a white feather standing.

"So you have come," he said to his wife. "Sit down." She sat down with her back toward the fire, facing the dark. The hunter then took out the dried meat and paper bread and put it in the fire for his wife to eat in spirit. They spent their first night there. As soon as the sun rose the white feather came up and started going again. The hunter followed it again until the sunset. There the white feather stopped again. The hunter did the same thing as the night before. He gathered wood and fixed supper. His wife spoke to him. "This time you will fix a small portion of food, because the night before you gave me too much of your food and I had a hard time finishing it." So the hunter put a small portion of food in the fire for his wife. They ate and talked to each other.

"Thank you for the food," said his wife.

The following morning the feather came up again, and the hunter followed it again. Soon they came to a place at the end of the mountain. There the wife did not want him to go any farther since he was still alive and not a spirit like her. She made the end of the mountain a steep cliff so her husband would not be able to go down with her. She had to stop him from going any farther. The wife, being a spirit, went down the cliff and left the hunter behind. He tried and tried, but he could not get down. He kept going from one side of the cliff to another, but he just couldn't find a way down.

He gave up and started crying. Toward the north there was a chipmunk playing around. He heard the hunter crying so he went to see if he could help. "Oh, my, I wonder why this person is crying. Something must be wrong." He came to where the hunter was crying and asked, "My dear father, why is it that you are crying?"

"My wife went down this way, but I cannot get down, and I am thirsty and hungry," said the hunter.

"Well, I'll go home now," said the chipmunk. "I'll see what I can do for you." Then he left for his house. When he got home he got a piñon nut, took the inside out, put water in the shell, and took it to the hunter.

"Here, I have brought you some water," said the chipmunk. The hunter looked at the shell and said to himself, "Oh, I'll just have to wet my lips with this little thing." But the chipmunk told the hunter that he would never be able to finish the water. So he drank the water. Meantime the chipmunk went back to his house and got a juniper seed. When he came back to the cliff he went down to the foot of the mountain and planted the seed. After the chipmunk planted the seed he went around and prayed as he planted the prayerfeathers on top of the seed. Right away the seed started sprouting and the chipmunk got hold of the top of the mountain where the hunter was.

"I think this is good enough," said the chipmunk to the hunter, "you will get hold of the top and pull it toward you. You will then get on one of the branches and start climbing down."

"Very well," said the hunter, and he did what the chipmunk had told him to do until he came to the bottom of the cliff. The feather had started going again and the hunter followed.

They had gone a long way and, since he still had a long life to live, again his wife tried to discourage him by making a great big cactus garden. She made all kinds of cactus so it would be impossible for the hunter to follow her. When they came to the cactus garden the hunter could not go any farther, so he started to cry. Later he realized that he had four pairs of shoes. So he put on one pair of the shoes and started over the cactus. Finally he came through the long cactus garden. His wife greeted him and told him, "Let us go on now." He took his shoes off and carried them on his back. They had not gone far when his wife thought again. "What can I do to discourage him from going with me, since he is still alive? I'm another person in spirit," she thought.

She finally decided to make a long trail of rocks, wood, and small trees so he would have a hard time getting through. She went over the woods, rocks, and trees as if nothing were in her way there. When the hunter came to this place he saw that it was impossible for him to get through so he started crying again. After a while he thought to himself, "I think you are trying to discourage me so I could turn back, but I am determined to go with you." So he tried and kept on stumbling over the logs and he finally got through. When he got to the end of the long trail of logs he saw the white feather that his wife wore on her head. "We will go on again," said the wife. "It is almost dark, the sun." They didn't go far when the sun settled.

"Well, we are here now," she said, "I shall soon see my parents, brothers, and sisters who have waited for me for so long. They will dance for me when I get to my destination. All my parents* are gathered here," said the wife. "I guess I will go there now."

His wife went ahead of him and they went to her parents' house. When they came to the house the houses were so small and there she met her parents who had gone before her. As she entered, she asked, "How have you all been, my parents?" She met her brothers, sisters, mother, father, uncles, and aunts. They were waiting for her.

"Very well, thank you," said the parents. Then right behind

---

* In life we have our parents who brought us into this world but when we die we have parents who are waiting for us in spirit. The parents mean older men and women who died before us.

the girl was the hunter who came in and greeted the girl's parents the same way the girl did, but the girl's parents did not talk to him since he was flesh and blood, so the wife told her husband to sit by the door at the entrance by the ladder. The girl shook hands with her parents and everybody in the room.

"Thank you, we have waited for you to come to us for a long time," said the parents to their daughter.

"I have come to you because of this certain bad person that shortened my life," said the girl.

"This is true," said the parents. "Why not sit down for a while? We will be going in a little while." They all sat and talked and then the parents told the girl, "We had better be going to the kiva where everyone is gathered and we will dance for you." As they left, the parents came first, then whoever had died next came right after, until it was the girl's turn because she had died last.

They left in a line and went to the kiva. Each took his turn in climbing the ladder into the kiva. It was the girl's turn to go up. As soon as she got hold of the ladder, her husband the hunter was right behind her, following her. But there was another person in spirit who got ahead of the hunter. This person in spirit was the first boy the girl had dated when they both had been alive. This boy followed the girl up and into the kiva.

The hunter just stood there watching them as they went into the kiva. Inside, the boy and the girl sat side by side as they had before she had married the hunter and the boy had died. The hunter had a hard time climbing the ladder. He kept slipping off the steps, but he finally made it to the top. Since the hunter was still alive, he had a hard time climbing the ladder; whereas the spirits had no trouble at all.

After the hunter climbed to the top he stood behind the door and watched his dead wife and her former boyfriend sitting there together. As he watched he started to cry. In the meantime there was an old owl nearby who heard the hunter crying and wondered, "I wonder why he is making himself cry. I guess I'd better go and find out." The old owl was on the north side when he heard the hunter crying, so he flew over to where the hunter was standing and asked, "So, you have come?"

"Yes, I have come," said the hunter.

"How come you are crying?" asked the owl.

"Because I want to go into the kiva but I'm not so sure, and my wife came here who died and I followed her," said the hunter. "When my wife came here she went up here, and as I was about to follow this other person in spirit went ahead of me. Now there they are, sitting side by side. What am I to do now?" asked the hunter.

"Really!" said the owl. "Do you love your wife?"

"Yes, I do," replied the hunter.

"Do you really and truly love your wife?" asked the owl.

"Yes, I really and truly love my wife, since we never had any harsh words for each other, now that she has left me and has gone to her parents," said the hunter.

"That is the way it is supposed to be. The very first person you happen to fall in love with, that will be the person you will return to after death. Even though you two were married, you weren't really hers. That boy she is sitting with right now, she belonged to him even before you two got married," said the owl.

"Is that so," said the hunter.

"Yes, that is the way," said the owl. "In life itself when you get married you are actually getting married to another man's girl," said the owl. Again the owl asked the hunter for the fourth time, "Do you really love your wife that much?"

Again the hunter said, "I do love my wife."

"Well, I'll be back. I'm going home and I'll see what I can do to help you," said the owl, and he left for his house. When he got home the owl prepared an arrow with bluejay feathers of its own. In doing this, if the hunter made a mistake by not waiting to get home with his wife and if the hunter made love to his wife, the wife would then turn into an owl, and the owl would win the girl.

The owl took the arrow and took it to the hunter who was standing at the top of the kiva. "Have the dancers come yet?" asked the owl.

"No, they haven't come, and I haven't heard anything yet," said the hunter.

"The dancers will come around on the south corner of the house and they will try out their voices. The man [priest] who is supposed to start the fire will come and when he bends down to start the fire in the kiva, you will shoot him in the back with this arrow. In doing so your wife will come back to you. She will become your wife once again just like before," the owl told the hunter.

As they stood there on the rooftop, the priest came. "He is the one who shortens our life when we forget that we are alive. You come once when you die even if you have a longer life," said the owl. "You will do as I tell you. That man will come and gather wood and will rub the stones together to start the fire. When he bends down you must shoot him in the back with this arrow I made for you to use," said the owl.

Sure enough, on the south corner of the house the dancers came, and they tried out their voices just as the owl had told the hunter. The priest came to start the fire; as he bent down, the hunter shot him, and the wife stood up, left her ghost suit behind, and came to join her husband. "So you have come to me, have you? Is it really true?" asked the hunter.

"Yes, I have come," replied the wife.

"Oh, thank you very much. My mother [wife], I had long waited for your voice. Even though I'm still alive, I came with you because I loved you very much," said the hunter to his wife.

"Very good!" said the wife. "You two must go now," said the owl. "You will go back the way you came. You will spend the four nights before getting back to your world. Your wife will live forever maybe!" said the owl.

"I'm sure I'll be able to wait until I get home, since I have waited so long to be with her," said the hunter, "and here in this spirit world everything is far different from our world where life goes on day by day."

"Yes, this is the way they live here in the spirit world," said the owl. "In life in your world the families live in fine, large homes. Each man and wife live in their own home. But here, after they are dead, they come back to their parents who have come before them. We are in one group, not scattered around as in your world. We live in small houses as you can see here. The roofs are made from willow trees and these are our permanent homes," said the owl to the hunter and his wife.

"Well, I guess we had better be going. Have a good day," said the hunter.

They hadn't gone far when the sun went down. This was their first night together. The next day they started off again. They went for a while, until about noon time. They sat down to rest and after they rested they started off again. They spent their second night without any trouble. That following morning they got up and started off again. In the meantime, the owl wondered how the hunter and his wife were doing, so he left to follow them. He got to a place called Fat Belly Mountain where he sat on top of that mountain. "I hope you'll follow my instructions and go by what I have already told you," thought the owl as he watched the hunter and his wife.

The hunter and his wife were spending their third night together, and next day they started off again. They came to a place called Athlabatsa where the wife wanted to rest. "Oh, I'm so tired, let us rest," said the wife. "We have come to our world now so we could sit down for a while. After we have rested a while, we can go over to our house. It isn't far now."

"Very well," said the hunter. "We will rest. You shall go to that other tree and rest there," said the hunter to his wife, "and I shall take this other one." So the wife went and lay down to try and rest, while the hunter did the same. The hunter kept looking over to where his wife was resting, all stretched out. Meanwhile, the owl was watching to see what they would do next.

The hunter just couldn't wait to make love to his wife. He got up and went over to where his wife was resting. "Now that we have come to our world it won't matter if I go over to my wife and hold her in my arms," said the hunter. So he got up and went over to his wife. There he lay down with her to make love to her. With surprise and excitement she jumped up and tried to say, "Oh, please, don't do that." But she could only hoot like an owl, because the owl had warned the hunter not to make love to his wife until they got inside their house.

"This is why I fixed the arrow with my feathers," said the owl. "I knew you wouldn't be patient to be with your wife. Even though when she was still alive you used to sleep with her, since she died, I helped you to bring her to life, but you just couldn't wait. Now the girl is mine," said the owl.

So the owl took his new bride and took her toward the west a little way from the Twin Mountains. That is why nowadays you can find owls in that area, since these two owls started their family.

34 Yellow Water Serpent's Head

A long time ago in the surrounding villages to the east of Laguna, there lived the two priest's daughters who never followed their father's advice or ways.

One day some boys went to the home of the priest and asked for his daughters' hand in marriage. They were told the decision was for the girls to make.

The girls said "Yes" and took the boys to their room, where they asked what they had brought. Then the girls told them the things they had brought were not what they wanted. "We would like to have the head of a Yellow Serpent. Our father needs this for his altar; that is why we want it."

"We do not think we can get it. The serpent is far away and it is dangerous. We may get eaten alive. I guess since we do not have the head, we shall go now." The boys left.

The next day, the mothers came and said, "Our daughters are coming over now, but the boys are not coming today. I wonder why they do not want to marry one of the priest's daughters. They must be saying something terrible to them."

The following day toward the evening while they were getting ready to eat, they heard a boy yell, "Say, come and help me."

The father got up and took the bundles of clothes from the boys and gave them to the mother. She placed the bundles on the floor while he was getting the other bundles. Then the two young boys came in and they both greeted, "My father, my mother, how are you this evening?"

"Fine," they all said. "Come in and sit down."

The girls got up and set some more places and invited them, "Now let us eat. We were about to eat and you must be hungry."

"Yes, we will eat with you." The two boys came and sat down on the floor with them to eat.

After they finished eating, their father sat down where he usually sat and told the boys to sit in front of him. The boys sat down and he began, "Now, my children, you must have come for an important thing, so you can speak up now."

The boys said, "We have come to ask you if we could marry your two daughters."

The father replied, "It is not up to me to say. It is up to my daughters."

"If you would like to marry us we will say 'Yes,'" the girls answered.

No more was said about the matter between the men and they sat there smoking and conversing. As it was getting late in the evening, the girls suggested, "Let us go rest now. You two must be tired."

When they had fixed their fire in the fireplace, the boys lighted the torches and set about to unbundle the clothes they had brought for the girls.

To their dismay, the girls said, "If you want to marry us, you have to give us what we want."

"If it is easy to get it, we will get whatever you want," one of the boys quickly volunteered.

"What is it you want?" asked the younger of the two boys.

"We wish the head of the Yellow Serpent."

"I guess we will not be able to get it," the boys said and told the girls good night, leaving with their bundles of clothes.

"My father, my mother, how was your night?" the girls greeted their parents in the morning.

"Fine, come on in and let us eat."

After they ate, their father went to his cornfield. Toward the evening, the mother said, "Girls, you'd better clean your room and the house, because someone usually comes every night."

The girls set about cleaning and straightening their house and created little jobs to pass the day with. When they were ready to eat supper that night, they had another suitor. "Oh, someone is coming."

"My father, my mother, how are you this evening?"

"Fine, sit down." Everybody greeted each other and sat down. The parents found the faces before them familiar. When they probed their minds about who they were, they recognized them as the sons of a priest from the village of Bin' Nawa'.

When they got through eating, the girls had the table cleared and the boys sat by the father and smoked. Being the sons of a priest, they knew how to smoke the sacred way, which was to pass the pipe in different directions and bless the people present in the room.

"There must be something you want or you would not have come," the father stated.

"We have come to ask for your daughters' hand in marriage."

"I do not have anything to say to that. It is up to them." The girls quickly answered and said it was all right.

When it was getting late again, they all went to the girls' room. There the two boys were told the same things the others before had been told. Again, the boys left with their bundles.

Then one day, the boys at Gyadetsi decided to go. The two brothers first told their grandmother that they would like to go marry the two daughters of the priest.

The grandmother said, "Oh, my grandsons, you will not do the right thing. You'd better not go."

But the two came on ahead. When they came to the priest's house, they yelled, "Hey, come help us!" And no one answered them. After the fourth time the eldest brother yelled and was heard. The two brothers proceeded inside.

"My father, my mother, how are you this day?"

"Fine," they greeted and the two went and sat down.

After this, they again sat down with the father and they asked to be married to his daughters. The girls looked at each other and made motions indicating the brothers were ugly.

When it became late, they said, "We will go to our room now." So they went out. Again, the two girls spoke of their father's wish to have the serpent's head for his altar.

The boys were supernatural and so they were unusually brave. This is why the grandmother did not want them to get married to ordinary persons.

"If you want it that bad, we will go and get the serpent's head."

They were ready to go the next morning. They got themselves the white shovels and got their bundles of food ready. Early the next morning, they left the priest's daughters.

Meanwhile the grandmother made known her anxious state. "Oh, my grandsons, what are you going to do?" she cried, but they had long left.

After a long distance the little brothers became tired and wanted to stop but kept on until they reached their destination.

They came to a place that was a village. "Let us see if the Yellow Serpent has gone home." They looked over the ledge and saw the serpent still lying around. Then they heard one of the serpents say, "I wish someone would come and put a yellow arrowhead in me. I have not been feeling good." The two brothers took off to find some yellow arrowheads in the ruins. They found one and the little brother also found a blue one for the Blue Serpent.

They went back and planned to kill them as they had set out to do. But because the boys were so sleepy and tired from their long day, they feel asleep when they sat down to rest a bit.

Early the next morning as the sun was ready to peek out, there were only the yellow streaks of light pointed to where the serpents had lain the day before.

They aimed the arrowheads toward the serpents and pulled the strings on their bows. In an instant, the serpents were killed and their bodies became visible again.

The two boys came to a small spring nearby where they washed themselves and became handsome. They put on the clothes they had brought and fixed themselves up.

They took the heads off the serpents and brought them along. When they came to the village, the brother suggested, "Why don't we put the heads down here and go this way?"

"Come on, we have to take these."

"We will be back," the little brother declared, so they went and as they looked over the hill, they saw a small house. It was lighted up from the flames from the fireplace.

They went on into the house and greeted the person, "My father, how are you this day?"

"Fine, how are you?

"Sit down," the father said and asked, "where are you coming from?"

"We were just passing by and we decided to stop in." The three conversed for a while and the brothers decided to stand.

The two went out and stood by a window where they made themselves invisible. The man, thinking they had gone, said to himself, "I had better eat and then make magic."

"What did he say?" the little brother asked in a whisper.

"Let us stay for a while. He said he is going to make magic. We shall see what he does."

So they sneaked around to a better view of the man. After the old man had eaten he got dressed in his white garment and put a rug down on the floor, where he sat himself. Then he said, "Now, this day my food is almost gone; therefore, I want white clay." And he clapped his hands and there was white clay. Then he hit himself on the right arm and there was gold clay.

That night after the moon had gone behind the clouds, the brothers took the white garments and the rug and left.

At sundown, they came to a few houses sitting on a hillside. Two girls came out and saw them.

The brothers said, "Let us go in and see what they would do to us." Curiosity led them into the house.

"Our mothers, how are you this day?" the boys greeted the two girls. "We saw your light so we came in."

"We are glad you came." The two girls put the meat on the floor and told the boys that it was meat from a cow. They also put down some paper bread for them to eat with the food.

The boys pretended to eat. When they had finished, they thanked the girls, and the girls cleared the floor.

"Let us rest now, but first, which one of you is the elder brother?" the older sister asked.

"I am," the older boy said.

"I will marry you and my sister will marry your brother," the older sister said.

"All right," the two boys agreed.

The girls fixed the beds and they lay down to rest. When the brothers pretended to be sleeping, the girls got up and went to the next room and brought long knives, which they quickly thrust into the bodies of the two boys.

Then they went into the next room and built a fire. "Now let us go and roast them." They deposited the bodies in a charcoal pit.

When they took the meat out, they were ready to eat. They heard some footsteps approaching.

"Come in," the girls called out. Two boys walked in and sat down where the girls were sitting there eating.

The younger sister noticed something familiar about them. She asked, "Are you not the boys that came last night?"

"Yes, we are the ones," the boys replied. "You are eating our flesh. You cannot live the way you are now. You have to stop." The brothers left, disgusted that there should be people like the two girls.

They came to another village by the cornfield and there sat down and went to sleep. After the sun had gone down, they awoke and went to a house where a man lived by himself. This man was another sorcerer. They decided to make themselves invisible.

When the man finished eating, he got up and got his blanket. He jumped on his rug and became a yellow horse. Then the horse jumped on his blanket and the man became himself again. Then he said to himself, "I will become a blue horse" and he jumped on the rug again. When he was through with his magic, he sat down. Then the boys came in as themselves and said, "My father, how are you this day?"

"Fine, sit down. You must be tired."

"Oh, yes," the boys said. "We are going around trying to find something to do."

Then the old man told them of the villages ahead where

they might find something to do. He told them of a place where they might be able to work.

The next day, they left and went to the place the man had told them about. They came to the edge of a village and saw all the people. They were gathered by a long pole in the center of the field.

One man was yelling, "Whoever is brave, come over and climb the pole."

The younger brother said, "I will go." And he did. He climbed the pole without any trouble and took a hat off the pole and the older brother got the magic shoe. When the people were distracted by another thing, the two brothers left with their magic shoe when they were sure no one was looking. A short distance away they came to another village.

"I feel like I want to go now. Remember we have our heads over there."

"Oh, yes," the younger brother exclaimed. "We have been out for a year now and we have not gone back yet."

The two agreed and left for home. On their way, they sat down and rested. While they were sitting down, they saw some people by an oak tree. The two decided to go over. The people were throwing a gold plate into a hollow tree. They said, "Whoever gets the gold plate out, gets to marry the governor's daughter."

The two went into the hollow tree and as the people started to cut the tree, the boys came out with the gold plate. They were told, "You will now go and marry the daughter."

The girl married the brothers, but she was keeping her acquaintance with a different man.

One morning on the day of the gods the girl said, "We will go to the meeting and talk to the people." So the two dressed and they went while the other brother watched them.

"My fathers, my mothers, how are you this day?"

Everyone greeted one another and the meeting started. When the meeting was over the people talked to their friends.

One night the wife wasn't feeling well, so she told her acquaintance to come to the meeting on the next day of the gods.

The two planned and at the next meeting they got together while the husband and his wife were in there. The boyfriend came in the form of a bird. He went around and around overhead and came and sat on the shoulder of the wife. Then after the meeting the bird left.

During that week on the second work day the wife invited the man and they visited with one another. The brother then put the magic shoes on and went in. The two of them were again planning what to do on the day of the gods.

After one of the brothers went in and went to sleep, the other brother came in and woke him up and told him of what he had seen and heard.

The next meeting day the wife left again and the boys got their magic pieces and went to the gathering.

The bird came again while the wife was playing around. The oldest brother got up and got the bird and threw it in the fire. The fire burned and the yellow bird became a black bird. Then the brother assaulted the wife and the two brothers ran putting their magic pieces on.

"The girls at home probably think we are dead."

When they left again they were tired, so they decided to stop and rest. The brothers finally got up and reached the place where they had left the serpents' heads. They spent the night there and early the next morning they woke up and left to marry the priest's daughters.

35 The Capture of the Runaway Shoomehcoolie

Many years ago when there were the villages of Hehshokda, Weemyahwa, Kyakima, and Kechipbowa, the villagers of Matsakya danced the Ahauda. Throngs of people from the farming clusters came to see the dancing.

At the same time there was one day left before the Yah Yah Dance commenced at Kechipbowa.

The Matsakya villagers wanted to see the Yah Yah Dance so when the Ahauda danced to their last song, no one requested that they dance any longer. That night the Ahauda Dancers returned all the borrowed jewelry and the parts of their costumes they had borrowed.

The next day all the people went to Kechipbowa to see the Yah Yah Dance.

Around noon, the dancers came out into the plaza and their leaders were instructing them to stand in their given places for the fourth time, when their masked dancer, the Shoomehcoolie, ran away.

With his white robes flashing through the forests onto the hills he was chased. Not far away a young man hunting deer saw the white robes flashing through the forest. At first the young man could not make out the figure, but as it got closer he thought about the Yah Yah Dance and the Shoomehcoolie that came out to dance with the dancers.

Sure enough, as the figure came floating through the forest, it was the Shoomehcoolie.

The young man hid himself behind a large tree in the path of the running Shoomehcoolie. Then in a moment the Shoomehcoolie was right behind the tree. As he passed, the young man jumped upon him from behind and they fell to the ground. A few minutes later the group of men chasing the Shoomehcoolie came upon them.

"Oh! Thank goodness you caught him."

The men returned to Kechipbowa and the Shoomehcoolie was taken to the Shoomahqueh Clan where he was ungarbed. Although the Shoomehcoolie was a supernatural being, because he had done this great wrong his robes and mask of the supernatural were taken from him and he became one of the ordinary.

The place where he had been caught was thereafter named "Shumingyah," where the Shoomehcoolie was caught.

To this day, there still rests in the heart of the village, under a building, a rock that is the very place recorded as the middle place.

The middle place is the heart, with veins reaching to the sacred Blue Lake, Tuba City or the Cotton Fields, Zuni Salt Lake, and Koh-thlou-wah-la-wah (near St. Johns, Arizona).

36 The Zuni Dances

Today as we live in the present ways of our people, we live also within the realm of our ancestors, for we are sustained through the rituals and beliefs of long ago. We live in accordance to the ways of our people, which bring life, blessings, and happiness.

It is a struggle to live with the most powerful of weapons against us, and they are the natural elements. For those of us who meet the end young in life we look unto the prayers, rituals, and religion in seeking life and its blessings.

As I tell you now, within the next few days there might come a time of religious ceremonial. Our children would be initiated into the Kachina cult to insure their life with longevity and happiness, for it is our belief that the Kachinas who flog the children pass on to them the life and blessing upon which our well-being exists.

It was once a ritual that took place in our lives regularly, for there sprouted six- and seven-year-olds, eagerly wanting to take shape into young men, and there too were the heads of the religious societies who took great care and were conscientious observers of the rituals. Within every four years when the Kokoh came from Koh-thlou-wah-la-wah, the initiation ceremonials would take place. But today there have elapsed many a time, long periods during which should have been designated the time to observe the rituals, but passed with not the slightest trace of ritualistic belief.

The Salimobiya circled the village, watched over their people for one or two days, and at that time we would be blessed by our protectors for it is their power that sustains life within us.

But as the many years have passed without the observing of rituals, we have made it a difficult task for the Kachinas, for our population has rapidly multiplied and our village has expanded to great proportions.

Now as we observe our people, we find it hard to pass unto our children what is known, but it would be a tribute to our ancestors if the people today would tell their young ones of these trifling but once important functions of their religion, not so much to exercise them but only to know what the Zuni have.

37 Adventures of the War Gods

A long time ago the War Gods lived with their grandmother on Towayalane. Early one morning after they had finished eating they took their bows and arrows out and they told their grandmother, "Grandmother, we are going out on the east side of here. We'd better go see our traps and hunt while we are out."

"All right," the grandmother told them.

They went out and went down to the mountain, across from their home, to see if they could catch some rabbits and other animals to eat. They took their lunch and were eating on some rocks at noon when the younger brother suggested, "Say, brother, why don't we go to the place that our grandmother told us not to go? Remember, last night? Come on, it won't hurt us if we only look," the younger brother said to his brother, who shook his head.

"We might get killed," the older brother said.

"We won't do anything to it," the younger said. So they went across the valley. There was a wild cow; everyone was afraid of it. Nobody dared to get close to the animal. Nobody went to the lake on the east side of Zuni even to get wood.

As they were hurrying along they saw a rodent. They said, "Oh! What is that?" They stopped in their tracks.

"What is what? It is just me," the rodent said, and crawled out of his hole. And he asked, "Where are you going?"

"Our grandmother told us that there is something over there that kills people and she told us not to go, but my brother wants to see it, so that is where we are going."

"If you go like you are now, you'll be sure to be killed. Come, I'll help you," the rodent said.

"How can we get in? The hole is too small," the older brother said.

"Oh," the rodent said, "that is easy. You just step up to the hole and the hole will become a door."

They looked at each other and then the younger brother stepped up to it and there was a door so they went inside. The rodent took them underground to the place where the wild cow was lying.

They went to the place beyond the dam. "Now you look at it from this hole," the rodent said. They looked out and it was a huge cow; it stretched a long way and was so high. "Now I will go out and take the hair off the place for you to shoot your arrow into. It won't do anything to me. I always go out in the morning and fix its fur."

"Oh, it's you. I'll go back to sleep," the cow said to the rodent.

After the rodent finished taking the hair off the place where the brothers were to aim, he went back into the hole. "Now I have made a mark in which you can aim." The brothers quarreled over which one should shoot it. The older brother shot it and it hit the heart and the cow made a big noise. As soon as they shot it they ran for the other hole, but before the younger brother got in, the cow hit him in the back with its horns.

He said, "Ouch! It got me!"

After they were in the hole the older brother said, "Let me see what happened to you." Then he faced him and said, "My! It is really bad."

The brother said, "Am I going to die?"

"Yes, you are," he told him. "You shouldn't have wanted to come here. Now look what happened to you."

They told the rodent and he said, "You're going to be all right." He took some medicine and put it on the brother. He yelled out since it hurt so much.

"What shall we do to it?" the younger brother asked.

"Let's cut it and see its heart." They cut the cow open and its heart was made of coral and turquoise and seashells.

"Oh!" they said. "This wasn't an earthly being! It is something else! Now, our grandfather, since you were so mean, since you were not good, since you were evil, you go now to where the sun goes up and the sun goes down. You go to your father. And because you were so mean you will become the Bow Priest of the father, the sun."

They let the heart go and then the heart flew to the sunset. "What shall we do now?" the younger brother asked again. At his brother's suggestion they took the legs and threw them into the skies, and they became stars.

Before they got home the younger brother said, "Please don't say anything to our grandmother. She'll really get after us!" And they agreed not to tell.

They climbed the mountain. As they entered the house their grandmother was cooking. They told her about their hunt—that they had got a lot of rabbits. Their grandmother thanked them for the good hunt. She fixed the table and told them to eat. The younger brother sat down on a rock they used for chairs. It hurt, so he got up and got a pillow and sat down on it. It still hurt and he was moving, trying to make himself comfortable. The grandmother noticed he wasn't sitting still. The younger brother looked at his brother and blinked his eyes as if to tell him to keep his mouth shut.

"Don't tell!" he whispered.

"What did you do? Why are you looking at each other? You must have done something!" She looked at them and they didn't say a word. "Did you go to the place I told you not to go near?"

The older brother said, "Yes, we did."

"What happened to you?" she asked.

"We killed it, the big cow, when the rodent helped us. But before we went into the hole the cow hit him in the rear and that is why he can't sit down," the older brother told.

"Let me see how bad it is." The grandmother took some medicine and put it on the War God.

He yelled out and cried, "That is enough!"

"This will teach you to listen to me," the grandmother said. Then a little while later it felt a little better so he got up and sat by the table and ate his dinner. While they were still at the table the grandmother said, "Now, my grandsons, I am going to tell you for just another caution. Don't you dare go over there to the south close to the nearest mountain. There is a big animal there that has a big bump on its forehead. It chases and eats people. This time for sure you might get killed if you go there."

"No, we won't go there," they told her.

"This time you'd better behave yourselves."

"Let's go play now. We'll remember what you told us," they said to her.

The next morning after breakfast they decided to go hunting again. "We are going toward the south and we will hunt by the trees," they said. "We haven't ever gone there."

"You'd better not go to the place I told you not to go," she said, while she was fixing their lunch.

"We won't go. Don't worry."

"You be sure to remember what I told you last night," she said as they were leaving.

They went toward the south by the big mountains, across the valley from their house. After hunting for a while it was noon again, so they sat down to eat their lunch. They finished their lunch and went back to their hunting. Later during that afternoon the younger brother suggested, "Let's go see the big animal our grandmother told us about."

"No, we'd better not. She told us all night not to ever go there."

"We won't hurt it," the younger brother said.

"Okay, we'll just look."

They went toward a canyon where it was narrow at the end; at the top of where they were standing was a solid rock with no way to get up or down. Then to one side they saw a big animal; it was a huge animal and it looked like their grandmother described it.

"Is this it?" the younger brother asked.

"I guess so," said the older brother.

So they whetted a stone at one end and threw it down. The big animal said, "Ouch! Who is throwing it? Come down!" They didn't say anything. They threw another one and the animal said, "Who is that that is just making fun of me? Come down!"

They said, "Let's go see what it does to kill people," so they got down and went to where it was lying.

"Where are you going?" the big animal said.

"We are going to hunt rabbits."

"There are a lot of rabbits around through there," the big animal said.

"Go on through," the older brother said to his brother.

"Where are you from?" the animal asked again.

They said, "We live by the Towayalane."

"Which one of you is the oldest?"

"I am."

"Go on through. There were some Zunis that went through, they will probably be coming now with their bundles of wood. I won't do anything to you," it told them again.

As the older one was about to go through, the younger one whispered, "Go on through, see what it will do to you." Just as he was going to go the animal kicked, but it missed the brother.

"How come you were going to kick me?" the older brother asked.

"No, I won't hurt you. I always get cramps in my legs," it said. It tried four times to kick him but every time it missed.

So the brothers took it by the feet and the animal said, "No! Don't do anything to me! I—" And before the huge animal finished what it was saying, they threw it down the side of the mountain. A few seconds later the animal hit the ground.

"Come on, we have gotten rid of it!" Then they went into the cave where it lived and there they saw a lot of things owned by the people who went to hunt and never returned home. "Oh, it must have been very mean," they said. They picked up their bows and arrows and returned home. As they were going the older said, "Now you be sure and remember not to say anything."

"You! You're always the one that has to say something first!" the younger brother answered.

"I won't say anything," the older brother said.

When they got home their grandmother fixed supper and they ate. While they were eating the grandmother was watching them. They were looking at each other and she noticed that something was wrong. "Oh, you two, did you do something again? You look so guilty. What happened?" she said. "I bet you went to the place I told you not to go."

"Oh, yes, we went," the older brother said.

And the younger brother said, "I thought you weren't going to tell."

"One of these days you are sure going to get killed if you

don't listen to what I tell you," the grandmother said.

"That big animal was fierce and it said it had cramps and tried to kick us, but it missed us so we pushed it down the hill."

"We killed it and we went to its house and found all the things that belonged to the hunters it had killed," the younger brother finished.

"Well, I am glad that you killed it. There were a lot of people that never returned from their hunting. Now, please, I tell you one more time before you go, not to go to the west side. There is a dangerous lady, Ahdoshla, there. She eats people and nobody ever returned. Maybe I am just wasting my words again, but don't go there."

They played the usual games again, then after the grandmother fixed the beds on the floor they rested that night. The next day they decided to hunt again. The grandmother fixed their lunch and they started. "Which way are you going?" she asked.

"We are going to the west side. We have never gone there before."

"Remember not to go where I told you last night," the grandmother yelled as they were leaving the house.

They looked around for a while and decided five rabbits were enough for right now. "Why don't we go to where our grandmother told us not to go?" the younger brother said again.

"You'll probably beg me to go anyway, so let's go." After they ate their lunch they started for the cave. As they looked over the corner of the mountain they saw an old lady sitting in the middle of the cave. This was the old lady that was dangerous that their grandmother had told them about. She was cleaning herself.

They threw a stone. "Who is that is hitting me? Come here! I will clean you up!" They threw some rocks. "Come on down!" she yelled again.

"Let's go see what she'll do." So they went down the mountain.

"Grandmother, how are you?" they said.

"Oh, my grandsons, where are you from? Which one is the older?"

"I am," the older said.

"Come here, I will clean you up." So the Ahdoshla lady was cleaning the older brother and she hit him on the neck and he went to sleep. "Now it is your turn," she said to the younger brother. She did the same to him and he too went to sleep. "Now I shall build a fire and cook the boys. For the first time in my life I will have some tender meat," the old lady said to herself. She built a fire and heated some rocks and when they were heated, she put the rocks on the two boys and then cooked them underground. Then she boiled some water and ground some corn. After a while the old lady took the boys out of the ground and put them on the table. She got ready to cut the meat. She sat down and said, "Oh, it has been a long time since I had a good thing to eat!" She got the knife ready and a voice came from the pot that she boiled stew in.

"That does not taste good, that is what I threw up." She heard it and got up and broke the pot.

"I have never heard of a pot talking," she said and sat down again.

Then she went back to the table and took a piece of meat she thought was the younger brother. She heard another voice, from the pot she baked her corn in. "I don't taste good at all!" She hurriedly got up and went to the pot and hit it until it broke.

"I never heard such things talk," she said. She went back to the table. When she was ready to eat, another of the pots talked, so she broke all her pots. Then the boys threw dust at her and it tickled her nose and she sneezed until she fainted and then she died.

"Now that is done, what shall we do?" they said.

"Why don't we skin her and make her look alive?" So they picked up grass and put it in the skin and sewed it up. Then they dressed it up so it looked alive.

"Let's go in and see what she had in her house," the younger brother said. In the first room they went into were a lot of things that had belonged to hunters. Then the next room had skeletons and skulls.

"Our grandmother the Ahdoshla was so mean," they told each other. The next room was bare. They saw a rock in the middle of the room on the floor.

"Let's see what it is." They took the rock off and the younger brother looked in and said, "Mmm, I smell something ripe like melons and vegetables. It is coming from down there."

"Let's go in and see. We'll drop ourselves in. I'll be first," the older brother said. So the younger brother held him by the arm and then he let him go and he dropped in. "Come on!" the older brother said after he landed a way down.

"Oh, brother, what are you trying to do? Have me killed?" he asked the older brother.

"Come! We have already landed!" he told his younger brother.

They looked around. "My goodness! It is another world! Which way are we going?" the younger brother asked.

"We'll go this way." They went for a little way and they saw the sun. That was where there were vegetables, melons, corn, and everything, and they were all ripe.

"There is smoke upon the mesa. Let's go up there." On the

way there were a lot of good things to eat as they passed by the fields. They picked up a few things and ate. Then they saw a lot of little people coming toward them, but they just sat there and ate while they were watching them. They talked to them but they couldn't understand each other. The people were talking like they had something in their mouths, so the brothers got their arrowheads and cut their mouths. After that they couldn't talk the same. The brothers told them to eat what they had in the fields and they ate. And it was the first time they had eaten. The little people were so glad: "This time you won't get killed," they told the brothers.

"One more thing," the little people said, "it is the great thing that boils." The brothers followed them over the hill and they pointed to it. "It boils over and if it drops on us we die."

The brothers looked at it and it was blue corn gravy. They said, "Let's eat it," so they ate.

"It there anything else?" they asked.

"No, that is all. We are glad that you came because now we can live in peace."

"We'd better go now, our grandmother is probably waiting for us." They left the village of the little people.

As they were going home to the cave that they had come into, they saw a big house. "Let's go see what it is. We'll just look," the younger brother said. When they looked in, there was some yellow pollen that went from the door to the sacred place, which was decorated. "Let's go in," they said. They went down the steps. "My fathers, my mothers, how are you this day?" they said. No one answered. "I guess there is no one here," they said. "Let's look at the pretty rocks."

"I wonder what it is for," the younger brother said.

The older brother picked up the stick that looked like a lightning streak. He squeezed it and it began to rain and then stopped. He squeezed it and it started again. "Oh," they said, "this is a miracle!"

The younger picked up a pretty stone. He rolled it and it made a noise like a thunder. "Let's take them," the younger brother suggested.

"No, we might get scolded."

"Come on, let's take it," he coaxed.

"All right," the older brother agreed. "Take the one that makes a rolling sound like a drum," the older brother said. "I will take the one that makes the rain." They took it and left the house.

They ran to the place where they had come in. The older brother went into the hole first and he reached for the younger brother. They replaced the rock as they had found it. "Now let us hurry," they told each other. "Our grandmother will be waiting for us, if we don't get there on time." They ran out and the younger brother said, "Oh, we forgot our grandmother the Ahdoshla." They turned around and went back to the cave.

"Let's place it behind you so that it would look like it is chasing you," the older brother said to the younger. "Now let's go. We'll fool our grandmother." So they hurried home. Just before the sun went down they got close to the house. The older brother said, "Now I will yell to call our grandmother. You pretend you are really getting tired of running, and she'll come down."

The older brother called for the grandmother. "Come on! The Ahdoshla is going to get my brother," he yelled. Their grandmother heard it and she looked out and the Ahdoshla was behind the younger brother. She got her stick she used to stir corn with and a long board she used to take the bread out with, and she ran down the mountain.

She met them and she beat up the dummy, and the boys

said, "Oh, that is enough. It is already dead. We killed her."

"You boys fooled me," she said as she laughed. They went laughing up the mountain to their home.

The next day the boys decided not to go any place so they went outside to play. "Brother, remember what we brought?" They went into the house and got a cloth that the things were wrapped in and they took them out. As they rolled the rock it made a thundering sound and then clouds began to form. But the brothers didn't know this. The other brother squeezed the lightning stick and made rain.

Soon they were having floods and their grandmother yelled out, "Come help me! The water is coming to my knees!" But they couldn't hear her. She yelled again a while later, "Come help me! The water is coming to my waist!" But they didn't hear her. They kept on playing. She yelled louder, "Come help me! The water is coming to my shoulders!" Then she gloated, "I guess they don't think about me. It is my turn to fool them," she decided. She hid behind the box in the next room.

The brothers saw the water pouring and they said, "We forgot about our grandmother. Take the rocks out from the windows and watch it. Our grandmother might float out of the window." So the younger brother watched while the older brother went inside to look.

"Has she gone out of the window?" the older brother yelled.

"No," he said.

"Come on in. The water is all gone. We have killed our grandmother. She must have drowned," they said and they cried. Hours later they began to get hungry. "We don't have anything to eat." They looked for bread and they found it in a box and it was all soaked up. They ate it anyway and they took a piece and threw it in the fireplace and said, "Here, Grandmother, eat. May you rest in peace."

Then the older brother said, "I would really like to eat an onion. I wonder if we have any. Why don't you look in the next room while I look here."

The younger brother said, "Oh, here is one growing already," and he pulled it. The grandmother said, "That is my hair." It was wrapped up in a green cloth. "You two boys, what did you do? You almost killed me!" she said angrily.

After the scolding the grandmother said, "This isn't the way we should live forever. We will have to separate, because it is meant to be our way. I will go to Halonaawa; there I will live with your grandmother and then whenever anyone wants a blessing, he can come to me and plant prayersticks. The older brother, you will go to the west. And you, the younger brother, you will go to the east. Each place will be remembered by everyone," the grandmother said to the boys.

The next day they went to the directions that the grandmother had mentioned to them. That is why we plant prayerfeathers there, to ask for blessings of rain each year. And they called it the place of the Ahauda.

38 The Rituals of Hunting

Many years ago our grandfathers, some of whom were in the Eagle Clan, often went out hunting, bringing back numbers of deer, antelope, and other game that they corraled near a water hole.

When they went out on such parties they came to the water hole, first setting up the corral. The corral had only one opening and just outside of this opening a tent was put up. Alongside the corral trenches were dug, with twigs and leaves covering them. Further on, out of sight of the corral, the men built a little shed for themselves. Around that, leaves were scattered. Then a hanger was built upon which the deer meat was to be dried. With prayers and sacred rituals, the trappings were blessed. In the corral, another trench was dug where prayersticks would be planted. By the time these projects were set up, the sun was setting, whereupon a paint was prepared that would lure the deer into the surrounding area so the men could easily come upon them. Long prayers and chants followed until they had all been said and sung.

Then the men began preparing the costumes they were to wear. White woven cloth was made into loose trousers and long shirts. That finished, the men retired for the night, anxious to carry on with the hunt.

Early in the morning they awakened and gathered their horses. After eating their morning meal they set out upon horseback into the forest to capture the deer. With the paint mixed the night before, they painted their faces. When they came across a very tall tree, a man took a post upon the tree overlooking the land.

On they went, for some time looking and scouting around. Upon finding a herd of deer, the men split up, usually into two groups of three. They then came at the herd from two directions. With two other men following, they approached the herd. Before long, the deer started running back and forth between the groups of men. The two men following made the sounds of another deer and soon the herd headed in the direction of the corral. Swerving back and forth the deer came on, and by luck and the spirits of the supernatural beings helping, the corral was full of deer.

With brush, blankets, and heavy poles the opening was closed. The leader of the herd would come forward and circle around in the corral four times and with a strong leap bound out of the corral. No one bothered to follow this buck, as it was thought that he had brought his children to their rightful place.

All of the men came, and the one chosen to kill the deer, dressed appropriately, entered the corral armed with a bow and some arrows. He carried out his duty, bringing down each deer until they had all been killed.

Each deer was bound and the men carried these to the shed from the corral; the blood mixed into the soil was gathered and bundled and put into a large rug and set aside. The corral was roughly cleaned. Upon returning to the shed, the men began to clean the deer and take the skins off. The meat was quartered and some cut up for eating and the rest cut into jerky, thinned, and hung out to dry on the hangers.

By sundown, the men ate and at night again set to work until all had been finished. Retiring for the night only to catch a few hours sleep, they spread out on the ground.

The next morning after gathering and feeding the horses, the men ate and dressed once more. With what was left of the paint, they again went out to hunt. Again the deer were sought and again herded into the corral and killed and butchered.

For four days at a time the men of the Eagle Clan went out for the deer. When the four days had ended, even though the deer were in abundance, the men would not pass the four days, for they believed it would not be good if they did. They believed if they did so they would lose their eyesight and become totally blind. When their work was finished, the men took down the corrals, the tent, and the shed and filled up the trenches, all with prayers of thanks. If they did not do this, the livestock, cattle and sheep, that grazed upon the land would not reproduce normally. They would all miscarry and eventually would die off because the prayers that had been said during the preparation of the corrals, the tent, the sheds, and the hangers would come to bring harm to these living animals.

And so with these rituals, the Zuni were sustained. Today the prayers remain with us, but the actual rituals of hunting are no longer practiced. This was the way of the Zuni Eagle clansmen.

39 Priest's Son and the Grandmothers

A long time ago there lived a priest's son in the village of Kwakina.

The village girls wanted to see the priest's son but they never saw him come out of their house. The surrounding villagers asked to have dances, because no one ever saw the boy and they thought the dances would lure him out to join the festivities.

At the same time, at the Salt Lake south of Zuni, the War Gods heard of this and they decided to talk to their Peyote brothers about trying to get the priest's son out so everyone would see him; so they started out for their home. When they entered, they greeted, "My mother, my children, how are you today?"

"Sit down, we are glad that you have come." The mother pointed to some rocks to sit on. "We would like to hear what you have to say because no one comes to visit us unless they have something important to say or ask us about."

"There is a boy who is the son of the priest, and he has never shown himself in public. We would like to have everyone see him. We will go and join the dances, hoping he will come out. We will take our grandmothers and have them dance with us. We will go now and we shall wait for you."

The next day, they told their grandmothers about the festivities and that they were to go with them. So the Peyote brothers told their grandmothers to go wash and get ready. After they washed they went into the next room where the old ladies became young girls, dressed beautifully. "Now we are ready to go see the War Gods."

"What shall we dance?" the girls asked one another, but were dismayed because they did not have a drum, so they decided to dance a social dance totally different from the rest of the regular dances. They started out and met a horned toad and he asked where they were going.

The four answered, "We are going to the village of Kwakina where we are going to dance."

"Can I go with you?" the horned toad asked.

They told him, "You are so old that you make a noise when you walk. Perhaps you should not go."

The horned toad suggested they use him as a drum, so after thinking it over they decided to take him. Before they continued, the horned toad was tried out as a drum. Indeed it sounded like a drum, so they fixed a stick for the drum and they were off.

Before they reached the village they stopped and decided to dance while entering into the village. When they did, the villagers saw them and looked out, and soon filed on either side of the procession. The horned toad then said, "Hit me hard, hit me hard, the priest's son is going to come out."

Then the priest's son came out and saw them. "I think I will go out farther and see who they are," he said to himself, so he walked out, soon getting between the girls.

The group had danced four times when the priest's son said, "Now, my fathers, my mothers, my children, I want to marry these two girls. There were a lot of people who wished to see me before this, but I never went out. Now that you have succeeded, let us go to my house."

"My mothers, my fathers, how are you this day?" The son greeted his family as the girls followed him in.

"Fine, sit down and eat," they were invited, and soon they were completely at home.

The War God spoke, "Now my grandmothers," he said, and hurriedly corrected himself and said, "My younger sister and our older sister, we will go now that you have been asked to be married to this man. We shall return to our home."

It was dark, so the priest's son suggested they go to his room and rest since they had had such a long journey. And so they spent the night together. The next morning he looked at one of the girls beside him and found that she was all wrinkled and old. He looked at the other and there lay a woman with white hair, old. When the two old women spoke up, one said to the other, "I am so tired, why don't you sleep by the fireplace?"

The other woman got on her knees and crawled toward the fireplace. The priest's son was disappointed and dejected as he left the room.

That morning the sister of the priest's son was told to go get the girls and her brother for breakfast. When the girl looked in she saw not the pretty girls but old women. She hurriedly went to her mother and told her that two old women were in the house instead of the two girls. "Tell them to come out and eat anyway," her mother answered, so she went back to call the two in.

Slowly, the decrepit old women made their way into the other room.

"My son, they have tricked you. They do not have lives like us. They are different kind of people," the priest said.

Meanwhile the War Gods at home wondered how their grandmothers were doing. "I wonder if our grandmothers have changed to themselves yet and I wonder what the priest's son thinks now."

Then the grandmother of the War Gods said, "My fathers and my children, if there is a man who constantly brags about himself, he will most probably marry a poor, ugly girl. If there is a girl who does this about herself, she too will marry a poor, ugly-looking man. Now call your Bow Priest," the little girl was instructed and so the Bow Priest arrived at the priest's home.

"My father, my mothers, how are you today? You may speak of what you would like to ask me."

"These people came and danced and my son, drawn to them, asked the girls to marry him and the girls are but old women. They are a different kind of people."

"We have not come to do harm. All we came to do is point out to these people that if there is a man who brags about himself or if there is a girl who does the same, they will end up marrying an older ugly-looking person who is with nothing. Now, we are not of your people. If you would fix a bundle of prayersticks to notify the people with, we would like to have cornmeal, turquoise, red Indian paint, yellow pollen, and black dirt. Notify the people to get the prayersticks ready."

With that, the War Gods went to the Peyote brothers and said to them, "Let us go get our grandmothers now."

The four went off. They arrived at the priest's house and were asked to sit down, whereupon they said, "Tomorrow you will give us prayersticks and we will take the prayersticks and return to our own land."

The old women, War Gods, and Peyote brothers were given food to eat the next morning and were given four bundles of prayersticks by the priest of the village, first to the War Gods, and then they began to pray.

"My fathers, my children, to your lands with our blessing you go to where you have won your place. Whenever the spring comes upon our land we will not be poor. The rains will always come and there will always be an abundance of water. There will be new topsoil washed out upon the land by the water holes. Our earthly mother, where the rains have made their marks, the holes will always be filled. Our earthly mother, with four blankets of blue, with flowers surrounding, with the surrounding lands of green, we give you these prayersticks to have. You ask for the rain spirits which bring blessings."

"So it shall be," the group acknowledged and continued the prayers.

"Furthermore, our fathers who have the earth toward the west, wherever you go, wherever you have won your place, my fathers and my mothers, our children wherever the shrine is, you will be known at the Peyote shrine for your blessing which we ask for. Whoever the owner of the earth may be, ask him that our land may not be poor, whenever the rain clouds form, whenever fog covers the earth, whenever your time comes, there will always be the passage way of the rains, there will always be water, wherever you stay.

"Furthermore, our earthly mother who has caused the erosion by the rains, may they always be filled. May there always be water upon the mountains all over. Our earthly mother, who is wearing the four blankets of blue, with flowers surrounding, with the surrounding lands of green, we give you these prayer-sticks.

"Wherever the land, wherever you originated, you ask for our blessing whenever you stop toward the south, where the Salt Lake is, there you shall meet your brother, we ask for you this blessing."

At that time the War Gods said, "So it shall be."

The people then sprinkled cornmeal on the four, and from this incident our people pray for rain.

40 The Cloud Swallower

A long time ago, it was at the Dry Lake where a man called Ash Drinker lived. There were some surrounding small villages and to the east, the War Gods lived with their grandmother atop Towayalane.

Early one morning while they were eating, the War Gods said, "After we finish eating, we will go fix our traps."

They had hunting traps along the Coney washes where they obtained much of their food supply. Their grandmother warned, "You can go, but there is something horrible at the bottom of this mountain. Don't you look or go there because he will get you."

"If it is something fierce, we will not look," the two assured their grandmother and continued, "Let us go now."

They departed and shortly came to the place. "I wonder what it is that is so great and fierce?" they wondered.

"We don't know and will never know if we do not see for ourselves. Let us go and see." Won over by curiosity, they went to the edge of the mountain. Once there, they looked over and saw something big and white curled up in a ball at the bottom of the mountain.

"What shall we do to it?"

"Let's give it a warning before we do anything so it may run away or it may come after us."

"How shall we do this?"

"We will yell for a time."

"You yell first then."

"I don't want to."

Finally the younger brother called and the white thing arose just a little. "It rose up a little!" the older brother exclaimed.

"Yell again!"

"It got up! Come on, some more!"

"It is getting up now!"

The big white figure stood up and looked around. "Yell some more."

The brother yelled again and the creature started to run. It went over the mountains in a few bounds.

"There might be someone over on the other side. Why don't you yell and tell them to send it back?"

Then their grandmother the bear heard this and said, "Who else could be here but me? There is no one else around."

She got up and stood with her paws in the air and growled.

The white thing turned around and headed back. "Now, brother, it is your turn to take its life," the younger brother said.

"No, I don't think so," the older brother replied. "I think you'd better do it yourself."

"Then I will. It is coming back now." The brother threw a turquoise weapon and it lodged in the creature's heart. And the cloud swallower fell to the ground. The weapon flew to a place by the Ash River. There was a flock of pigeons drinking so their feathers were cut away from their legs by the turquoise weapon, whereupon the pigeons came to have red feet. Then it went to where the bear lived.

The War Gods yelled again. "If there is anyone behind the Ash River, stop our weapon. It is heading there."

Their grandfather bear heard this and he knelt down before the weapon as it hit him on the back.

The War Gods went over and looked at the cloud swallower and it lay stretched, covering a large space. It was huge.

The grandmother approached her grandsons and asked, "Did you take its life?"

"Yes, we did, and that was for the best."

She replied, "Many of our Rain Gods have gone out into the clouds and they never returned. This creature must have been the cause of their disappearance. It is not an earthly being."

"Now it may be that every one of our children on earth, wherever anyone wishes for our father's weapons, our earthly children, you that will follow and live after your fathers, this will be the place to ask for blessings of hunting."

"This will be the place," the grandmother acknowledged. "They will plant prayerfeathers and fast to thank the one that made this be."

"Now you will tell us what to do."

At that, the bear sang a song and told them, "This is a song of a blessing to whoever might have the heart or spirit to hunt. And if they come here and ask for blessings, they will have something to bring into their homes."

Before the men go to the Salt Lake, they cut prayersticks and when they reach the lake they plant these prayersticks. Young men go into the lake to help gather the salt. After the young men return who were at the lake for the first time, a ceremony is held at their home by their aunts—it is a ceremony of purification.

41 Story of Salt Lake

Once there was a Salt Lake up at Black Rock where the Salt Lady lived. Our people at that time had very poor sanitation. The Salt Lady did not like being polluted with trash and debris, so she moved away from there. She moved to the southeast, going through a rock in the mountain, now known as the Pierced Rock. Continuing, she went through the forest. The path she took is very clear along the side of the mountain. Going down through a canyon she came to a lake where she established her new home.

The people who lost her began searching for the salt. They made their prayersticks and the Head Priest and another started out riding donkeys. They traveled all day, and the following day they came upon her. There they planted their prayersticks, praying for forgiveness for being so careless about keeping the lake clean and beautiful. Then they took some salt out of the lake and started home. Coming to the Ahauda they made another prayer. Since the Salt Lady had gone in that direction, they called the south Salt Lake, or Mahgyayaqueh.

They traveled for about two days and three nights. Early the fourth morning, they came down into the village. The people shouted and cheered, calling their names out.

As soon as they reached the village, they went to their homes where their aunts anointed them with the washing of their hair and hands. When the aunts had done as they did, a portion of the salt that had been brought back was given to them as tokens of appreciation.

Following that, a special prayer would be made to the Salt Mother that she keep bearing fruit for the well-being of the people around her.

VI WAR AND DEFENSE

42   Lonkeena and the Horse Thieves

Long ago, when the Zunis lived at Ojo Caliente, they held horse races each day. During one of these races, there came two white men who happened to be outlaws. When these outlaws found out that one of the Zuni men named Gethlakkaye had lost the bet in one of the races, they told each other to help Gethlakkaye in betting against the Zuni men.

The Zunis had won twice before, so they knew which horses were the fastest. The Zunis were willing to bet against the two outlaws. One of the outlaws took the saddle off his horse and helped Gethlakkaye with this. But even so, they lost the bet. So the other outlaw, the one with the wooden leg, bet his horse against the Zunis to help Gethlakkaye, but lost again. Finally, the outlaws bet what they had with them, meaning their bedrolls and their clothing, but again they lost. By this time, the sun had gone down into the horizon.

That same night, the two outlaws swept off with all the horses the Zunis owned. The horses were around the Hawikuh area with their front legs tied to prevent them from running away. The outlaws cut the ropes that bound the horses' feet and took off with the herd. The outlaws had taken the herd toward the west, along with their own horses.

Not far from the village of Ojo Caliente, somewhere around the area where the willow trees grew, there was a young man who was herding his sheep. The night the outlaws took off with the horses, the dogs at the sheep camp kept barking. To the sheepherder, the dogs were barking at some stray horses—the wild horses nobody wanted. But these wild horses turned out to be the horses from Ojo Caliente village that the outlaws had stolen.

The next day the Zunis ate before attending to the matter of their stolen livestock. After breakfast, several of us started off to round up our horses, but to our surprise, we found no horses in sight. The only things in sight were the ropes we had used to tie the horses with the night before. We didn't bother to put our horses in the corrals in those days. There was no need to put our livestock in pens or corrals.

There were a few horses at the village of Ojo Caliente. We gathered those horses and formed a searching party. We put on the saddles and gathered what weapons we could find at the village.

It was during the time of famine. There was hardly enough food to go around, so we didn't think of taking the food with us. We had no other choice but to go on and hunt without food. As soon as we got to where the willow trees grew, we spotted the tracks. We followed the tracks until we got to where the sagebrush grew near the little cave. Here at the cave we discovered that the outlaws had stopped here to eat and rest. After eating, the outlaws had continued on to Gasudoomo road, which is south of Ojo Caliente. A little way from this road are the black layers of rock. Around this area lived a few families of the white men. There was a road going up to these black rocks where the white men lived. When the outlaws got the horses up on those rocks, they continued toward the west mesa to where there was a wagon trail down the mesa. That is where the outlaws let the horses down. And here was the place where we came down.

Out in the clearing, there stood a horse belonging to one of the men at Ojo Caliente. The outlaws left it behind because the horse had been injured along the way. One of the men in our party named Baelthna [Cayalito] told the rest of the men that he was going to take the horse to ride on.

"That sore on the horse doesn't look very good, but I guess you can take it," said one of the men.

"Yes, it sure doesn't, but this is the best horse and I'll take the chance," replied Baelthna. "I've heard that this horse never tires." He saddled up the horse and we started off again, still following the tracks. Since there were so many horses, the tracks were easy to find and follow. Toward the east, along the black layers of rock, there was a ledge where we found Epaloose's spotted horse and a gray mule. In rounding up the horses, the outlaws must have overlooked these two animals, so Kaweuka went up to get the horse and the mule. Epaloose saddled his own horse up and now the party needed three more horses. Kaweuka's uncle, Baelthna, told him, "You must take some of these horses and head back to Ojo Caliente. We don't need all these horses." So we continued on toward the west until we came to a house owned by a white man named Salamona. Here the tracks showed that there was a horse with horseshoes, which went toward the house and there were shoe tracks of a man from the house to where the horse stopped. The man on foot must have been talking to the other man riding the horse.

None of us knew any English and the man Salamona knew a little of the Spanish language, so Baelthna talked to Salamona in Spanish. Baelthna asked Salamona about the horses but Salamona gave Baelthna a different story, so Baelthna turned to us and said, "We had better go now. We have stayed here long enough and wasted enough time. I am sure the white man will not tell on his friends. Let's go." So we proceeded. We hadn't gone far when we heard Salamona calling, so we turned back to the house. When we got there he asked, "Do all of you men have rifles? When you catch up with those two men, kill them because outlaws are no good. They will have to die. I am going to give you these two boxes of shells to use to kill the two outlaws."

We went on our way until we came to a settlement called Atarke. South of this settlement along the black layers of rock lived a Mexican man with a patch on his eye. Here Baelthna talked with him about the outlaws for a long period of time but he didn't reveal anything to us. Up to this point our searching party was big enough, so some men stayed behind because not all of us had rifles. Tsiadelalusie, Tsewahde, and Tsebo were the ones who stayed behind with the rest of the men. Those who had rifles and went on were Walela, Epaloose, Diama, Wyaco, Tzaleshe, Baelthna and Wanaowluhuh and myself [Lonkeena]. Eight of us continued since we had the rifles.

None of the men knew the country except for one man, Baelthna, who was our only hope. He knew his way around this part of the country. The rest of us followed Baelthna.

As we continued on our journey we came to some hills which they called the White Hills. Here we discovered some eggshells and saw where a fire had been built. Baelthna got off his horse to examine the ashes and the ashes were cold. The outlaws must have spent the night here. All along the way, the outlaws had been leaving a trail of tracks and places where they had stopped to eat.

We pushed on until we came upon a windmill where the outlaws had watered the horses. We continued until sundown. It must have been in June, since the moon was in its first quarter at that time. We traveled on until we came to a water hole with hills surrounding it, then we went up. When we reached the top of the hill, Baelthna stopped and motioned to us to stop also.

"How come you are stopping?" we asked.

"Well, east from here I see something moving. I am going there to see what it is. When I get close enough to see what it is, I'll start shooting if it is the outlaws. If they have their camp there, I'll look for them. As soon as I locate them, I'll start shooting. When you hear me shooting, you be ready, and come as quickly as you can," instructed Baelthna.

Baelthna didn't wear fancy Levis or any store-bought pants. He had on white pants and a white shirt. He took off his shirt and rolled up his white pants above his knees. He loaded his rifle and took off toward the east.

Meanwhile, the rest of us started looking around to see if we could see what Baelthna had seen. Of course none of us saw anything. Baelthna had real good eyesight and so far he had proven to be a very good scout for the searching party.

Baelthna had thought he had seen the horses. As he neared the herd, the herd ran off, but they were cows. So Baelthna returned to us, informing us that what he had seen was a herd of cows. He put his shirt on and unrolled his pants. Just before he got on his horse Baelthna had another thought.

"You men stay here," ordered Baelthna, "I smell smoke. The outlaws must be spending the night somewhere around these hills. I'll go and check to the west of these hills to see if they are there." So off he went in the dark toward the west.

We started sniffing in all directions but we couldn't smell anything. Baelthna must have had a sensitive nose and a good sense of smell. When Baelthna got to the top of the hill, he could see far into the distance some more hills that ran in all directions. But there was a hill that extended toward the east and on to the south corner of the hill, and there was a place like a gorge. Here, it has been said, our forefathers wiped out the Navajos.

For some odd reason, Baelthna could see the fire, so he thought that the spirits of our forefathers were around those hills, tipping him off about the outlaws spending the night somewhere around there. These hills were steep like the Hawikuh hills.

As this fire lighted up, the rest of us could see it too. Baelthna came back and asked, "Did you see that light?"

"Yes, we did. It came from that same place where our forefathers wiped out the Navajos during one of their battles," we replied.

We got on our horses and started off toward the hill where we had seen the fire. We came to the dried riverbed that was called Burned River. Here we could see the tracks of the horses and where the outlaws had gone. We followed the tracks until we came to another water hole where bushes and sagebrush grew. Then Baelthna told us to stay behind and take cover.

"South from there, there are three houses. I'm going there to check them out. Since it rained, the outlaws will have to take to the houses and dry themselves before moving on. If they do, I'll be there, but if they're smart enough, they might be with the horses right by the corral gates. If they're there, I'll start shooting. On the first shot you men start coming," Baelthna ordered us. He rolled up his pants again, took off his shirt, and went toward the house while we waited eagerly.

Baelthna went over to the corral and saw that nobody had spent the night there. East from the corral stood one of the houses. Baelthna put his rifle on his back and crawled over to the first house. When he reached the house, he removed his rifle from his back and then he stood up. Edging his way to the window, Baelthna listened for snoring but there seemed to be no one sleeping there. He went around to the door and went inside the house. He found no one there either. Then he went to the middle house and again there was no sign of them. He went on to the other house, but he found no one there. He left the houses and went down a little way only to find a water hole. Since the ground was wet around the water hole, Baeltha could see the horse tracks very easily. After making sure there was no one around, Baelthna made like a who-do-do to let us know that there was nobody at the house.

"Let us go now," said one of our men. "He must have found no one there."

So we went on over to where Baelthna was standing, still imitating the who-do-do.

"They're not there. They didn't spend the night there either," Baelthna told us. After Baelthna got back on his horse, we started off again. Before we got to where we saw the big fire, the moon had disappeared into the horizon. After the moon had disappeared, we lost the tracks. However, Baelthna went on even though there was no more light. He just went, thinking and hoping that he was on the right trail. None of us wanted to get ahead of him. Nobody knew the way, so we just followed Baelthna.

We went on and on until we reached the place where our forefathers had killed the Navajos and where we had seen the big fire. There was a spot where the trees grew in one big bunch. We decided to stop and rest for the night. We unsaddled our horses and we tied their legs. What were we supposed to eat? Nothing! Nobody had anything to eat. Baelthna turned to us and asked, "Oh, please, doesn't any one of you have anything to eat?"

"What were we supposed to bring to eat? There is a famine and we were all starving—nobody gave us anything to eat," said one of our men.

Yanaowluhuh replied, "I have two pieces of tortillas in my bag." He took them out and gave each one of us a small piece. We were hungry because the last meal each of us had eaten was when we were still in Ojo Caliente. After we ate our small pieces of tortillas we sat down to smoke.

"Doesn't anyone have any tobacco?" Baelthna asked.

"Why, of course not! Who would think of gathering the stuff you are supposed to take when we were in such a big hurry," replied the men.

"Well, I have just a little bit left in here somewhere," said the late Epaloose. He got it out for us, then Baelthna said to us, "Every one of you make your own cigarette."

We each made our cigarette. After we made them, Baelthna and Wyaco put a blanket over their heads, making a tent.

"When we light the match, you will light your cigarettes one by one under this blanket," Baelthna told us. So we did just that. After all the cigarettes were lit, Baelthna and Wyaco came out from under the blanket.

"Every one of you will hide your cigarettes as you smoke so no one will see the light or know we are here," ordered Baelthna. We did what Baelthna told us to do. After we finished our cigarettes, we got ready for bed.

"Let us go to bed. We are tired since it's been a long time ago that we started from Ojo Caliente," said Baelthna. "Maybe tomorrow we will be able to catch up with the outlaws and our horses by following the tracks. About noon we will leave the horse tracks and go straight to Silver City. If we're lucky, we'll beat them to that town, or they might be there ahead of us," said Baelthna.

War and Defense

We didn't know where Silver City was. None of us knew where we were going to be heading. We were tired, we just wanted to get some rest. Before we went to bed, Baelthna told us, "You will get your rifles ready and put them where you can reach them in case the enemy attacks. We will all sleep in a roll and not be scattered about." We all got in a roll like Baelthna had told us. We made our beds with saddles for our pillows. We were very tired; we went to sleep in no time.

Walela, Epaloose, Wyaco, and Yanaowluhuh, the four of them, got up in the middle of the night without waking the rest of us and went toward the south, away from the camp.

"Now let us look for the horses. We'll see if we can locate them anywhere," they said.

The three men got Yanaowluhuh ready with medicine that made him foresee the future. This man saw two little supernatural beings and these beings told Yanaowluhuh, "My fathers, my children, our livestock, tomorrow when our Father the Sun comes up, you will catch up with your horses." Somehow, Yanaowluhuh didn't see the two horses of Epaloose—the white one and the red one. The reason was that the outlaws were to run off, riding these two horses after the attack.

"While you men are going in that direction, I shall go this other direction to see if they backtracked us. If I find them first, I'll shoot once and you should come quick. You just listen for that one shot," Baelthna told us.

So we saddled our horses and started on our way. We went over two sets of hills and headed toward the east. Baelthna, going his way, was looking for horse tracks but he couldn't find any. Baelthna was on foot, while we were on horses. Somehow Baelthna got to those pine trees before we did. When we got close to the pine trees Baelthna was waiting for us. He was imitating the who-do-do, informing us that he hadn't found anybody in his search. When we came to him, he asked, "Are you just now coming?"

"Yes, we are," we replied.

"We have to wait here because when I came here I saw somebody lighting a match. Maybe this is where they are spending the night. We just have to wait here," Baelthna told us.

Sure enough the fire lit up while we waited, and we could see a man walking around the fire. There was a wagon with high railings, kind of red in color. When we saw it from that distance in the darkness and the light coming from the fire, we thought that it was a house instead of a wagon. As we watched, a man ran toward the east hills and then back to the camp fire.

"I think we have finally caught up with the outlaws," Baelthna said. "The horses may be toward the east hills in the clearing and that's why that man went there to see if the horses were still there."

"We must wait before we attack. We'll wait until dawn," Baelthna told us. "Just as soon as there is enough light, we'll attack. I'll go first and we'll go in a single file. And you two [Lonkeena and Walela] will be the last ones to follow. When we get to those outlaws, maybe if they don't get mad and don't fight or shoot at us, we will each shake hands with them. You two, you're young and strong, when you shake hands with them, get hold of them so we can help capture them. Before we get close enough, maybe they will start shooting, since they're outlaws and have done wrong. If that should happen, we will shoot back at them. If any one of you should run, you mustn't run straight on. You should run zig-zagging so the bullets will miss you. Get your rifles ready for firing," Baelthna told us.

So we went on toward the outlaws' camp, our brave one being the leader, and Walela and I at the end of the line. Walela and I were still young at that time, but the others were much older. When we neared the camp we could see the fried bread and bacon being fried and the coffee already prepared. When the man saw us, he just sat there scared to death. His hands were shaking as he held a cup of coffee. Our brave leader Baelthna spoke to the white man in Spanish but this man didn't understand that language. The man spoke to us in English, but none of us knew anything of that language. We all had a hard time understanding each other.

The white man got up and made sketches on the ground of a sunset and pointed to where the outlaws had eaten, and where the fire had been built. We could see the smoke and the horse tracks. The man told us that the outlaws were going to spend the night close to the mountain.

"We must go now since we have spent a lot of our time here," Baelthna said. So we got up and left the camp. We hadn't gotten far when Baelthna decided to return to the camp where we had seen the food. We followed him and did whatever he did. He took the fried bread, bacon, and coffee, and we helped him gather the food. We left nothing for this white man except the dishes.

We rode on, eating what we had taken from the camp. On we went to the Shado Mountains, where you would find rocks that are formed into bowls. We went into the gorge that led to the Shado Mountains, and here we saw more horse tracks. At the end of the gorge, toward the east, there were lava beds where the horses went up. We followed until, at the top, we lost the horse tracks because there were too many weeds and rocks. The only thing left to do was to follow the waste the horses had left behind the day before.

On we went, over two hills, and on the second hilltop we could see a mule in the distance. Tzaleshe and Walela followed the mule's tracks until they came upon the two men saddling their horses. Before we could warn Walela and Tzaleshe, the two outlaws spotted them. Right away the outlaws got on their horses without realizing that they hadn't finished saddling their horses. When they rode off we saw that one of them had a wooden leg, so we were sure these were the two we were after.

Before the outlaws could get away from us, we started shooting. The echo from our shooting sounded all around, since the ground was still wet from the rain that had come the day before.

On the first round of shooting, the outlaws were knocked out; however, we kept shooting, not giving the outlaws a chance to shoot back. For a long time we kept shooting. We didn't know the outlaws were out cold. When the outlaws came to, they saddled up and rode off, shooting at us. When they started shooting, the rest of us ran off and hid. Yanaowluhuh and I ran off together. We ran in the direction of the hill, and about halfway up the hill there stood a big tree, where we hid. The tree was big enough to hide us both.

Our brave one kept firing as he chased the two outlaws toward the Shado Mountains. At these mountains, at the east corner, there was a trail where the outlaws could have gone, but they decided to go up the east hills instead of going up the trail at the east corner. They were riding the white and red horses that belonged to Epaloose.

When they reached halfway up the hill, they dismounted from the horses and used the horses as their shields. Baelthna was right behind them, just a few yards away. The two outlaws fired at Baelthna but the bullets just grazed Baelthna's nose. So Baelthna got hold of his horse's neck and rode off, hanging on to the neck, and then he turned back.

Yanaowluhuh and I just sat there watching the fight, not knowing whether to join in or not, and as we sat there, bullets came flying around us. As the bullets hit the tree trunk, we could see the smoke coming out from the outlaw's rifle barrel. Baelthna turned and rode off toward the north. The wind was coming from the north and it formed a hump on the back of Baelthna's shirt as he rode off.

The outlaws kept on firing bullets at him. When they fired, they missed his body, but they got the shirt where the hump was, making holes in the shirt Baelthna was wearing.

All the firing from the rifle shots made the horses uneasy. They ran around like they were going to stampede. The horses came toward where we were sitting, so Yanaowluhuh waved to the horses to scare them, and for the horses to go in a different direction, which they did.

Baelthna wasn't about to give up hope, even though we weren't helping him. He turned around and kept firing at the outlaws.

At the top of the hill, right above the two outlaws, Wyaco appeared. The outlaws didn't notice Wyaco approaching because they were too busy firing at Baelthna. They weren't expecting any one of us to join in because they knew we had gone to hide.

Instead of shooting Wyaco just yelled down at the outlaws to get their attention. "Hey! You no-good outlaws. Look up here," yelled Wyaco. When the outlaws found that they were surrounded, they mounted again and rode off, along with all the other horses. The herd went toward the mountain along with the outlaws, but then the horses turned back. The outlaws led their horses up the trail as they kept on firing at Baelthna. By this time Baelthna was wounded but he hadn't given up yet.

The outlaws got away when they went over the mountains, so Baelthna came back to where we were. When we saw him approaching, we went to meet him. When we came face to face with Baelthna, he looked horrible. During that fight, he got himself wounded when the bullet grazed his nose. His face was covered with blood because of his wounded nose, and there was white foam in the corner of his mouth. When he stood before us, he asked, "Oh, my children, aren't you two scared of how I look?"

We just stood there looking at each other since we didn't fear the sight of him. We were too young to know how it felt to be in a battle. We saw what had happened to Baelthna, and up to now I can still remember.

"You two must be brave at heart," said Baelthna to us.

By this time, the outlaws were safe on the other side of the mountain. While all this fighting took place, Tzaleshe was at the camp where the outlaws had kept their belongings. Tzaleshe was busy unfolding the blankets while the bullets flew past by him. He put the blankets on the saddle, along with the hats, spurs, and leather pants. He also gathered the sacks of flour and sugar and a box of crackers. The rest of us were trying to round up the horses in the clearing so we could change horses, but the horses wouldn't settle down because of all the excitement.

"We have to go back the way we came. We must build a corral with those dried-up pieces of wood I saw way back there," Baelthna ordered. We went back and gathered the wood and made the corral. We rounded up the horses again and then we put them in the corral. Ever since we had left Ojo Caliente we had had the same horses up until then. We had to rest the poor horses before they gave out.

After all that excitement, none of us was hungry or thirsty. We changed our horses and had sat down to rest when Tzaleshe showed up with the stuff he had gathered at the outlaws' camp.

Baelthna was angry at Tzaleshe. He said to Tzaleshe, "What

did you think you were doing? You knew very well there were bullets flying all around us, one of those bullets could have killed you. You were stupid to be unfolding the blankets during the fight." They stood there looking at each other; then Baelthna said to him, "You were lucky you got here safe." Then Baelthna went over to the horse and unloaded the blankets. The rest of us joined in and we grabbed for the blankets, spurs, and hats. Just as soon as Walela and his in-law, Epaloose, dismounted from their horses, they grabbed for the leather pants, sugar, and a box of crackers. Tzaleshe had the sack of flour, but not for long, because Diama came running over, grabbed the sack of flour, and ran back to his horse. Now Tzaleshe had nothing left.

"We must go now, since we have gotten our horses back," Baelthna said.

Diama asked, "Could somebody help me round up those horses? There's the black, red, and a gray horse that belongs to the outlaws. They're over there at the lava beds."

"Do you really want to go gather the horses?" Baelthna asked.

"Why, of course," Diama replied.

The late Wyaco agreed to join in with Diama to help round up the other horses.

"Just a minute," said Baelthna. "Come over here. I want to talk to you two." So they came over to where Baelthna was standing.

"If you two really want to go, you may. When you have gathered the horses, you can put them in this corral that we have already made," Baelthna told them.

"Remember we came over two hills back there. When we get there we will go toward the west and we won't wait for you two. I'm afraid of the Burned River Village because the outlaws might have gone there for help and those Mexicans will do anything for pay. If the outlaws get help they might come back here and it won't be good for us, so we can't stay here," Baelthna said to them. With that said, Wyaco and Diama rode off to round up the horses.

Baelthna turned to Walela and me and told us to round up our men's horses so we could move out. Walela and I went to do what Baelthna ordered. We came to the first hill, and Baelthna said to us, "Get the horses together before they go off again." At the first hill Baelthna called to Diama and Wyaco, but they hadn't come in range to hear Baelthna's call. No one came so we pushed on. On the second hill, Baelthna ordered Walela and me to go gather the horses. While we were gathering the horses, Baelthna called to Diama and Wyaco, but no answer came, so we left, heading toward the place where we had been the day before.

"Now let's rest and wait for Diama and Wyaco," Baelthna said. "You and I will stay here and wait for them," he said to Epaloose.

"I don't want to stay," Epaloose said.

"Of course you're going to stay here with me," ordered Baelthna.

"But I don't want stay here. I'm going with the rest of the men, on down the hill," pleaded Epaloose.

Baelthna got mad and grabbed the reins of Epaloose's horse and held Epaloose back. While Baelthna held Epaloose back, Tzaleshe, Walela, Yanaowluhuh, and I, the four of us, went with the horses down the hill.

Just before we left, Baelthna told us, "You go now with the horses. If Wyaco and Diama don't show up and if those outlaws have gotten help at Burned River Village, they might just decide to come back here. If they come, we won't follow you. We will warn you as we take cover among these ledges. Let go of the horses and take cover over there among those mountains. See that white mountain? It will be safer there. You will have to find a place where you think you would be safe." Our hearts were pounding furiously as we went down the hill with the horses.

Meantime, Diama and Wyaco rounded up the horses, but they didn't put them in the corral. Instead of going the way Bealthna had told them, they headed on to Burned River Village.

Since Diama and Wyaco hadn't shown up, Baelthna and Epaloose came galloping over to where we were. He told us that Diama and Wyaco hadn't come. We went to those three houses and at the corral we put the horses in, then changed horses.

"We won't stay here at these houses. We'll go to that place where we were last night. It's that hill over there," said Baelthna and pointed to the hill. "Maybe if the Mexicans help the outlaws, they will come here to these houses," Baelthna told us. We took the horses and left them up ahead toward the direction we would be going in case the outlaws came. We were on top of the hill where we could keep a watch. Our stomachs were growling from hunger. We ate the crackers and sugar from the outlaws' camp.

Baelthna said, "Look over there. See that mountain which comes from Burned River Village and at that end of the mountain, right about where Kyakima is? That's where the outlaws would appear if they have gotten help from the Mexicans. We should be able to see the dust. There is a desert that has at least five hills. On the fourth hill, if you can see the outlaws, you must give me all the ammunition you can find and leave it with me. Then you will take the horses and head on home. I will try to hold them back as long as the ammunition lasts. If I'm lucky and if I don't get shot, I'll live. When my bullets run out, I'll tell you. You must then run for your safety. Take cover if you want to live. You came through that part of the country and you should know where to hide."

Well, we had come through that country, but at night, and we weren't sure what kind of country it was. We were still eating when we saw a cloud of dust coming from the place Baelthna had told us the outlaws would come from if they had gotten help. But it turned out that the cloud of dust was not from the outlaws, but from Diama and Wyaco. They had gone to Burned River Village and asked for help. They had sold one of my horses, the red one, to get help. They wanted the Mexicans to take them to the Red Mountains because they didn't know that part of the country. At Burned River Village, the governor gave his boys bullets and rifles. He told his boys to take Diama and Wyaco straight to the Red Mountains. While they were at the governor's home, he gave Diama and Wyaco some liquor. By the time they left the governor's house, Diama and Wyaco were feeling high.

At a distance, we could see that there were many of them and we thought that they were the outlaws. As they came near we saw there were two of our men, three of the outlaws' horses, and two of the governor's boys. We kept our positions as we watched them. They came over the first hill, then the second, third, and fourth. On the fourth hill, as they came down, we got our rifles ready for firing. Then on the fifth hill, as they emerged, the two of our men called to us in a long yell. The two Mexicans turned and headed back to their village.

When Diama and Wyaco came with the three horses that belonged to the outlaws, we went out to meet them, to take the horses away from them. Walela grabbed for the red horse,

Diama got hold of the black one, and Wyaco took the gray horse.

The outlaws got away with Epaloose's two horses, so he had lost his horses. After they had changed horses, we started out again. We came to a place where a Mexican man had been hanged. We were going very fast, and this made foam form around the horses' mouths. Before they reached the Mexican's house, Epaloose said, "Let's slow down to a trotting pace because I have something to say." We slowed down to a trotting pace and Baelthna asked, "What do you have in mind?"

"Well, we have come this far with Tsiadelalusie's horses, and he had more than any of us. Over there at the Red Mountains, we should sell two of his horses. If we get a large sum of money, we should divide it among each of us. This is what I had in mind," said Epaloose to Baelthna.

"Is that what you had in mind?" Baelthna asked. "Well, I won't do it. Maybe if you had helped me in fighting the outlaws, I might have gone along with your plans. But because of me, we have gotten our horses back. If I wasn't with you men, you would have gotten as far as that place where the Mexican man lives. There you would have lost all these horses.

"No, I'm not going to sell any horses. If we did sell any horses and the people found out, we'd be in trouble and we'd have to pay for the horses we sold," said Baelthna.

Then Walela came forward to his in-law, Epaloose, and said to him, "Look here, Epaloose, you have no shame at all. Because of you, we ran off and hid while the fighting took place, and now you think you're going to claim everything."

As we rode, Walela kept scolding Epaloose. Then Wyaco went to them and said, "Will you two stop arguing for a while?" Then he told us to stop. We came to a halt and dismounted from our horses. Here Wyaco blessed and sanctioned us from all evil. After he had done that we went on.

Just before sunset, we arrived at the Red Mountain Village. All the Mexicans there knew about us going after the outlaws, so when we entered the village, they all gathered around us. There was this young man who gave Baelthna a hard time and he called us all kinds of names, including "wolves."

The governor came and got hold of this young man's jacket collar and said, "There were two of you living here. You two were no good and you had a large herd of horses, cows, and sheep. You sold them in order to get out of jail or pay off what you had stolen. You sold your livestock to get drunk and that is why you two are poor." Then the governor just kicked this young man around. After telling him off, the governor took us to his home. There he fed us hard bread. Since we were very hungry, we ate the hard bread as if the food was going to vanish.

After we ate, the governor gave each one of us a small bag of tobacco, paper, and matches to make cigarettes. He also gave us a gunnysack full of dried-up bread. As soon as Baelthna put the sack of bread on his saddle, we started out again toward home. As we came on home, we had to spend the night at a place called the Powdered Mountain.

Epaloose, Walela, Wyaco, and Diama built a fire so big you could see it for miles.

"Why are you building a fire that big?" we asked.

"Who would follow us? We left a long time ago," they questioned. Epaloose, Wyaco, Diama, and Walela were sound asleep before long. The four of us stayed up, Yanaowluhuh, Tzaleshe, Baelthna, and myself. We didn't go to sleep because we had to guard the other four men and our horses. Baelthna kept us awake by telling us about his adventures. He told us that he had gone on war parties against the outlaws many times. We had to chain smoke in order to stay awake. The next day our lips were burning and hurting from the tobacco and the smoke.

Baelthna told us that he had killed at least ten outlaws and gained a lot of money because the outlaws had money with them. That's why he was never broke, he always had money.

"When you kill a white man, that man wouldn't put up a fight as he is dying, because they are weak at heart and die fast. But if you kill an Indian, that Indian would kick around before he dies, because an Indian is hard to kill," Baelthna said.

Then he changed the subject and said, "My children, this is what has happened to us [meaning the fight for our horses]. We have fought for our horses. When we get back home, there's this man named Black Beard, don't tell him anything of what has happened to us."

He also told us not to tell Black Beard about the white men's horses.

As we rode on, Epaloose turned to Diama and asked for one outlaw's horse so that he could team the one he was riding with the outlaw's horse and use them as working horses, but Diama refused Epaloose's request, he wouldn't hear of it.

However, Epaloose didn't give up. He kept on bothering Diama about the horses as they rode on. Finally Epaloose said, "But you are poor and have no money to pay whoever comes and tries to get the horses away from you. Before you know it, they will take you to court for horse thieving."

Every so often Epaloose would ask Diama for the horse. Finally, Diama got tired of it and gave up all the horses to Epaloose. After Epaloose got the horses, he went to Black

Beard to have him draw up legal papers of ownership.

"You must sign some papers for me because if the outlaws should want to claim the horses, I think I have the right to their horses," Epaloose told Black Beard.

Black Beard drew up the legal papers for Epaloose so that he would have proof of ownership of the horses. When Black Beard did this, Epaloose in turn told Black Beard about what Baelthna had told them not to tell. Since Epaloose hadn't helped in the fighting, he told about the blankets and all the belongings that we took from the outlaws. Then he told Black Beard about the saddlebags that the outlaws had. He also told them that they didn't look in the saddlebags and that there might have been some money in them. No one wanted to go back there again because we were scared of those Mexicans and because we didn't want to fight anymore.

After Black Beard signed the legal papers, he sent them to Fort Wingate, where at that time the soldiers were still stationed. It took only a few days before the soldiers arrived at Ojo Caliente. The soldiers wanted to take one of us who had been there, to guide them. None of us wanted to go back and risk our lives. Nobody was willing to take another chance.

The late Diama and the late Tsewahde took the soldiers to where we fought. For one whole month they searched that place real good, but they didn't find any bodies of outlaws.

"If Walela hadn't come from behind the outlaws, they could have been dead by now," Baelthna said. "It was possible for me to finish them off if Walela hadn't shown up from behind," said Baelthna.

For one month, the soldiers stayed at Shado Mountains, searching for the outlaws' bodies, but they couldn't find them because the outlaws weren't dead.

This is what happened a long time ago.

43 Zunis and the Navajos

In the old days when the Navajos lived not very far from the Zunis they were forever raiding the Zuni village.

The Navajos from the area around Oriole Lake had decided to have another raid. Among them a young Navajo lad heard about the preparations for the raid and was not in favor of their plans. He listened as plans were being made for the attack on the Zunis. Then he came to inform the Zuni Bow Priests.

When the Bow Priests of Zuni received word of the attack they informed their people of the planned attack and advised them to prepare for it.

"We will go to the dry gulches on the outskirts of Zuni. In the gulches we will set up to wait for the raiding party. The raiding party will surely come to the village first. There will be a few people left in the village. When the Navajos come these people will flee toward the gulches. There they will join our forces and wait for the Navajos. As soon as they come into the gulch we will be prepared for them. From all directions the Navajos will be attacked," the spokesman said to the villagers.

He asked if the Navajo boy would come along with the warriors. The boy replied, "No, I am not coming. I came to inform you because I don't believe in fighting. I did not want you to be caught unprepared and murdered."

The Zunis prepared their weapons and two days after they had been informed most of the Zunis left for the gulches where they were to wait for the Navajos.

Shortly, the Navajos came and the remaining villagers fled from the village, running into the gulches with the Navajos following them closely. When the Navajos entered the trap they were attacked from all directions. The fighting ensued until dusk and still neither party gave up. Through the night the furious battle raged on.

Only one Zuni warrior was wounded. The rest fought until the Navajos were driven into a tight corner, and there the whole party was slaughtered. Scalps were taken and a man named Gehdah was made a Bow Priest. The scalps were brought into Zuni and Gehdah's initiation into the Bow Priesthood was celebrated.

44 The Navajo Warrior Kethlnakai

Long ago when there were Zuni villages at Ahmossah and the Blue Well, the Navajo warrior Kethlnakai lived with his people near what is now known as Fort Defiance. Boowhoshkeeshe, his raiding partner, was also close by.

Kethlnakai spoke to his friend, "We will go on a raid to Zuni. But first, we will speak to our people. The two villages at Ahmossah and at the Blue Well will be our prime targets. If we are lucky and if we pull through the battle, we will take many handsome lads and many pretty maidens as captives. We will bring back their jewelry and seeds of survival as our own. Now," he asked, "what do you think about my wishes?"

"What can I say about your plans? Since you have set your mind to the great plans, I can only follow you as I am dependent upon you and you are our leader."

"Well then, you will go out to the neighboring settlements and inquire about their views. See if there are any objections to the raid. If no one objects, I will give you the word to begin and we will then rise against the Zuni."

So Boowhoshkeeshe went about and inquired as to how the others felt. The Navajo generally agreed saying, "We have no objections, as many a Navajo dreams of having Zuni captives as their slaves."

When Boowhoshkeeshe thought there were enough Navajo who had endorsed the raid plan, he returned and told Kethlnakai, "There have been no objections and there are enough to go raid the villages. When you have decided when we are to start out, I will go out and tell the people."

"Well, if there are enough to go out already, today, I will tell you. Seven days from today, we will meet at the Cracked Rock, and everyone shall meet. From there, we shall go down to Ahmossah, where we will raid the village. And the other village we will raid later because if we come in to the Blue Well village first, word of the raid will reach the other villages and they will unite and rise against us. When we have all gathered we will spend the night there and early the next morning, we shall raid the village."

So Boohwhoshkeeshe went out once more and told his people their instructions. Then during the seven days, weapons were repaired and strengthened.

Came the seventh day and huge throngs of Navajo came to the Cracked Rock where they went over their plans until everything was set.

Early the next morning, the Navajo started out before anybody in Zuni had awakened. They came up to the willows, down to the Clay Spring, and along the Oriole Ridge on into the village. When the Zuni were attacked, they wasted no time in gathering their weapons. Soon after, the Zuni began fighting back and the battle raged on in the small village.

As the Zuni men soon numbered equally with the Navajo, they fought relentlessly and the Navajo began to retreat. The villagers at the Blue Well soon received word of the attack and armed themselves, coming to reinforce their neighbors. When they did so, the Navajo were trapped between the two groups of Zuni.

As the Zuni shot arrows back and forth and injured some of their own, word was sent to the villagers of the Blue Well to come join the people of Ahmossah.

So the Zuni were then combined into one huge group and soon the bodies of many dead Navajo lay on the ground.

Kethlnakai the Navajo leader spoke, "We will retreat now. We have to retreat. We cannot go by our plans. We have not taken any captives but we must retreat."

The Navajo fled up north with the Zuni chasing them only a short distance behind. And as soon as the Navajo had gone over the red hills, the Zuni turned back for home.

When the Navajo reached their home, the leader spoke once more, "Many of my people, my relatives, our elders we have lost in the battle. This will have been the last time I went on a raid to Zuni. Because when we go to raid Zuni, we do not return with glory and satisfaction. When we do go, during the battle there have always been two small boys going back and forth during the fight. I have become scared and wary of them and now I will stop going on raids. This is all I will go out anymore. If there should come someone with the desire to go on a raid against the Zuni, it will be up to you to decide. If you want to go, go ahead. But because I have lost and suffered much, I will go no more."

The Zuni took the scalps of all the Navajo that had fallen in the battle and left the bodies in the scorching heat of the sun.

A few days later, what few Navajo survived came with wrappings to recover the bodies of their dead. They solemnly took the corpses back and the same day, Bylause and Keshcooli became priests because of their bravery.

When Kethlnakai stopped coming to Zuni, all was quiet until the sons of Tzuni, another Navajo warrior, were all killed. Tzuni came to Kethlnakai asking his aid in an attack of the Zuni village.

Kethlnakai refused adamantly and spoke his words of wisdom, acquired from his experience of attempts to raid the villages. "I will not go to raid the villages of Zuni, because even what you think are your best horses or weapons do not perform as expected. The horses do not run their speed. The warriors are unsure of themselves. I have gone to Zuni to raid the villages of the Blue Well and Ahmossah but I returned with no captives and I am never going back again. If you want to go, go ahead, but I will not go."

Tzuni went about the Navajo settlements and again many Navajo wanted to go once more to Zuni, hoping to take captives and bring back the valuable possessions of the Zuni. When there was a great band of Navajo ready, they came upon Kethlnakai for the third time, asking if he would come so there would be great strength among them. But Kethlnakai refused. "I will not go. I think too much of my people to lead them to destruction, because for some reason the Zuni, even down to the smallest and youngest, fight with the strength and confidence of many strong men and we are inferior to them."

But Tzuni kept prodding Kethlnakai until the man told him, "I do not want to go and hereafter I do not want you to come around bothering me."

Tzuni went off still not convinced that the great warrior did not want to go to Zuni to capture some young Zuni for a slave. So a couple of days later he returned, not paying heed to what he had previously been told.

"I have come after asking you to come with us several times. I cannot think you would refuse to go to Zuni to capture the young lads and pretty maidens, who would be of great service to you. I think you might have changed your mind after thinking about the great possibilities lying ahead for us."

"I will not go and I have told you many times now, I will not change my mind. For when the Zuni are attacked, there appear two small boys who may be the source of many victories. No, I will never go. If you want, go ahead. Even if I do want Zuni captives because I have lost many of my people, I cannot repeat the same mistake again. The Zuni have powers which we do not have and even if we kill them, it would only be one or two. They will not be defeated. When we relied upon the word of one who is supposed to be a great warrior, we lost many of our men. Therefore I will not go again. Do not return after a few days thinking I will break down, because I have said I will not go."

Tzuni started off and turned back and asked, "You will not go then?"

"No, now go. When you have gone, I will await your return to see what you bring back."

"Yes! And you will see what we will take from the Zuni. I go now."

Navajo from all the surrounding settlements gathered and they went to raid the village. The Navajo came just outside the village when the great cloud of dust rising beneath the thundering hoofs was discovered by the Zuni and immediate action was taken to fight the Navajo off. The Zuni gathered at the corrals and waited while Tzuni atop his white horse came bounding up to the waiting Zuni. He tried to hold his horse back, but it went on instead, until only a short distance away he was dropped from his horse.

The Zuni went out to meet the Navajo and soon fighting led the Navajo to the west, where more Zuni emerged to fight. On to the village at Blue Well the Navajo were pushed, until they were again surrounded. As they barely managed to flee to the north, the Zuni kept up with Navajo falling to their deaths, and as one tried to recover the bodies, he too was soon among the dead.

The few survivors were left to head back to their settlement. Kethlnakai soon observed the warriors straggling in, greatly reduced in number and leaderless.

"So you have come back. Now where are the lads and maidens you have captured?" His tone a little gentle now, he told the warriors, "Let this be a lesson to you all."

True to his word, Kethlnakai never again rode in battle, but lived his days out among the relatives surviving the battles of attempted raids.

45 Doowhooli

In the days of old up in the Blue Mountains lived the great Navajo warrior Doowhooli, and a short distance away by the Oriole Spring, another warrior, Yellow Beard, lived.

Both these men owned large herds of sheep, but Yellow Beard was not content with what he had. Therefore he spoke of going on a raid to Zuni. He approached Doowhooli and the warrior agreed. "Then we shall go."

"Yes, now we must speak of our decision for all our people to hear."

The two warriors went about with the plans of their raid. No one objected or raised question of what might happen. Everyone was eager with anticipation at the thought of gaining possession of many valuable belongings of the Zuni.

"When will we be going?"

"In four days we will depart on our journey to the village. We will not take the village of Yellowhouse first, but instead we will go to the mountain villages located above the spillway. We will go through a small settlement in the valley on our way down."

After a day of preparation, the Navajo started out at once. One of the young men had refused to go, but he waited until the others left before he started out as an informant to the Zuni village. He cut through the plains on directly down to Kechipbowa.

When the Zuni discovered the Navajo, they wanted to kill him but the Sebuloutche [Betrayer] talked his way out, telling the Zuni, "No, do not kill me. I have come to tell you a great party of Navajo warriors is coming within the next two or three days. They will come to destroy your village. I did not want to come with the people so I have come alone. Do not pass these days without doing anything in preparation for the attack, for you are the prime target. Now that I have told you, I will go."

Because the Navajo, any Navajo, were considered enemies, four Zuni men had gone out of the village to a small ravine where they waited for the Sebuloutche to come by.

Not long after he had told the Zuni, the Navajo was on his

way back home, when the Zuni men attacked and killed him.

    The Zuni began their preparations in anticipation of the raid. Two days passed quietly and the third day the Navajo attacked during the early morning hours. The villagers each morning had waited on the outskirts of the village. As the Navajo came upon them, they made their way back to their village and on over the hills onto a small lake upon a small hill. When they came upon the hill by mid-morning, the villagers of Hawikuh a short distance away took notice of the battle and immediately set out to help the people. As the Navajo continued pressing the Zuni farther back, the Zuni from Hawikuh were dispatched for the farther village of Uumbassah where the men quickly gathered and came from several different directions surrounding the Navajos. As the fight came on to Hawikuh, a great many warriors met them head on, and the Navajo retreated.

    The Zuni shortly outnumbered the Navajo almost three to one. Taking advantage of their strength, they chased the Navajo, killing them off relentlessly until the Navajo came upon some small hills and went over them. The Zuni turned back when they saw there were but a few Navajo left and the rest all lay dead on the ground.

    The few survivors went on home, stopping shortly at the Oriole Lake. Doowhooli, who had lost all but a few of his men, was asked by Yellow Beard, "What shall be done now? There have been many of my people lost but I want to form another group to go back."

    "I do not know. Even if I told you to go ahead, it will not make any difference to the Zuni. They are stronger and we seem to be weaker than they so I cannot tell you what to do. As has happened before, if I did tell you and something went wrong, you will only flaunt the mistakes upon me," Doowhooli replied.

"I will wait then. I will go out among our people and see if they will join forces with me. If they will, I will come back to tell you."

"So be it."

The warrior went about the villages that surrounded the Blue Mountains but there was none who wanted to go back to Zuni with them. The ones that had gone before remembered the figures of two small boys always running between the two warring tribes. Each time that they have been observed when they stay within the Zuni warriors, their enemy has no chance of fighting back enough to have any effect on the Zuni.

But Yellow Beard went ahead and got together a few men from distant settlements and started out for one of the small farming clusters of Zuni. He did not inform Doowhooli of his intentions of assuming the responsibility of avenging the deaths of many of their Navajo warriors.

Yellow Beard came on with his party, stopping at a red clay gully, where one of his followers asked, "Exactly where are we going?"

"Over to the Blue Well where there is a small village. If we are lucky, we will succeed in avenging the deaths of our fellow Navajo. What will be, shall happen," replied Yellow Beard.

Then the brave announced, "I will not go then. You go on ahead if you wish."

"So you will go back then," and to the party, he stated, "if there is anyone else who would prefer to part from the rest of us, be on your way."

Yellow Beard with fewer men rode on to his mission, but after only a short way his partner approached Yellow Beard with a request to stop a moment so he could bring out his thoughts to be considered.

"What shall be done?" asked the partner, continuing, "I do not think our chances are very good. I have looked at our number and there are but a few of us. The village we are going for is a little larger than we can handle. I have given much thought about our people and there remain only a few alive. I think we should not continue any farther. We should turn back now. I leave the decision to you."

"So you have spoken your thoughts. I thought only about the people Doowhooli lost to the Zuni and my desire to carry out the vengeance I have built within myself. But it is true that Zuni do not think of themselves during battle. They are far braver than anyone who has come against them. We have proof enough to show us this is true. We have lost a great number of our people to them."

Yellow Beard paused for a moment and went on, "I too think it would be best for us to turn back, for it is not good when there is conflict among us. If I should persist in going while you object, great danger might fall on us and more will be lost. You have convinced me to go back with you."

The Navajo party turned back after coming as far as the lake outside the village of Hawikuh. Quickly they returned to their settlement where Yellow Beard explained, "We turned because we did not think we had very good chances of fighting. We looked at our people and there were not enough of us. It was good my partner brought this out and we decided to turn back. We have returned with our people safe and unharmed. What we decided we thought to be best, for no one knows what will happen for sure. And the Zuni are brave and stronger than the Navajo. Only when great numbers of Navajo come do we take the lives of two or three Zuni, leaving many of our people dead at the hands of the Zuni. Now that I have realized what we are up against, I will return from going on raids. If there should be anyone desiring the knowledge of the ways and rituals of warriors, I shall pass my knowledge unto them. My medicine and war chants, I shall depart with for the benefit of other warriors."

"No, you cannot do that, because your knowledge is precious. The medicine and war chants, no one else shall know the rituals of a warrior," the Bow Priest announced.

Yellow Beard then announced to his people, "Now, all my people, I have returned with you. No more will we go out on raids. I have retired now. What I know will be useless to me but I will keep my knowledge."

From then on, the Navajo from and beyond the Blue Mountains ceased altogether coming on raids to the Zuni village.

46 Apaches Raid Zuni

There were many conflicts in Zuni because of jealousy and suspicion, causing much suffering and hardship to the innocent people.

A man who thought himself to be treated unjustly went to the Apaches and told them that the Zunis planned to raid their settlement. The information was false, but nevertheless the Apaches were angered and they planned a raid on Zuni.

Four days after they had been informed, the Apaches rose against the Zunis. As they came, they came upon a small field early in the evening. Not very far from the field on a small hill they put up camp for the night. Later, down in the field, they saw a fire light up.

The Apaches decided to wait until night came before they went down to the field to see if anybody was camped there.

Only a short time passed and darkness fell over the land. And the Apache leader instructed two of his warriors to go scout around in the field. "If there is anybody around, tell them to go where his people are. If he has any melons, bring one here."

The two left with their instructions. They went toward the fire and looked to see if anybody was there. No one could be seen, so the warriors eagerly went into a small garden where they found plenty of melon and other crops.

They brought to their leader one melon as they had been instructed, and were told to crack it open. The melon was divided among the warriors. Before it was eaten, part of the flesh from the melon was prepared into a paste, then used as a war paint. When the melon had been eaten, the paint was applied to the warriors. "Now we will be ready early tomorrow morning. We will be ready to attack." A fire was built in the camp and all went to bed.

About five miles west of the Apache camp, a lone house sat ablaze with fire from the fireplace within, lighting the openings of the house. There in the house a woman lay writhing in the agony of childbirth. The relatives awaiting the birth patiently sat in another room. A young man got up and left the house for a walk to get some fresh air. He saw the fire from the Apache camp.

He immediately told his family of what he saw. "There is a fire on a hill not far east of here. They might be Navajos. We should send word to Zuni for them to prepare themselves for a possible attack."

A man was sent with his instruction to Zuni. There the priests were told and they immediately called out to their people, advising them to stay within the village and ready their weapons for a possible attack.

The night passed without incident and soon it was dawn.

At the very first crack of dawn, the Apaches came down from the hill. They came into an arroyo and followed it down until they were only a short way from Zuni. They came out from the arroyo and attacked the village.

The Zunis had done as they had been advised and so it took only a minute for them to organize themselves and start fighting.

The Apaches thought it would not be hard to overtake the Zunis but were surprised to find themselves battling a furious fight.

As the Apache leader retreated onto a small hill south of Zuni, he looked back and saw two small boys riding horses in the middle of the battle. The Apache looked at the two boys intently and thought he imagined them appearing and disappearing on the battleground.

Alarmed, the Apache leader called to his warriors to retreat. The warriors retreated to the north. They came to a cliff where a large rock hung over, making a small cave. In it, they found the two boys sitting around a small fire.

"Do not harm them, they are not doing anything," the Apache leader ordered.

They went on above the cave and stopped there. Looking back, they saw the Zunis coming behind them, gaining time. Again the Apaches went down going east, not stopping until they reached their country.

The Apaches realized their strength was surpassed by that of the Zunis, so they did not try to raid the village for a long time.

It is believed that during the raids against Zuni, the spirits of the War Gods, or the two little boys often seen playing about amidst the fighting, were the protectors of the Zunis and the cause of the victories won against many raiding parties.